VI

Introducción a la lengua española | **FIFTH EDITION**

Santiago Canyon College
Library

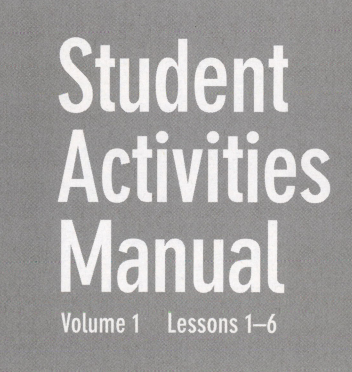

Student Activities Manual

Volume 1   Lessons 1–6

VISTA®
HIGHER LEARNING

© 2016 by Vista Higher Learning, Inc. All rights reserved.

ISBN: 978-1-62680-745-7

4 5 6 7 8 9 PP 20 19 18 17 16

Table of Contents

Introduction   v

WORKBOOK

Lección 1   1

Lección 2   11

Lección 3   23

Repaso: lecciones 1–3   35

Lección 4   37

Lección 5   49

Lección 6   59

Repaso: lecciones 4–6   71

VIDEO MANUAL

Fotonovela Activities

Lección 1   1

Lección 2   3

Lección 3   5

Lección 4   7

Lección 5   9

Lección 6   11

Panorama cultural Activities

Lección 1   37

Lección 2   39

Lección 3   41

Lección 4   43

Lección 5   45

Lección 6   47

Flash cultura Activities

Lección 1   79

Lección 2   81

Lección 3   83

Lección 4   85

Lección 5   87

Lección 6   89

LAB MANUAL

Lección 1   1

Lección 2   7

Lección 3   13

Lección 4   19

Lección 5   25

Lección 6   31

Introduction

The VISTAS 5/e Student Activities Manual

Completely coordinated with the **VISTAS** student textbook, the Student Activities Manual (SAM) for **VISTAS** provides you with additional practice of the vocabulary, grammar, and language functions presented in each of the textbook's eighteen lessons. The Workbook and Video Manual sections will help you continue building your reading and writing skills in Spanish. The Lab Manual section will help you continue building your listening and speaking skills in Spanish. Icons and page references in the **recursos** boxes of the **VISTAS** student textbook correlate the Workbook, Video Manual, and Lab Manual sections to your textbook, letting you know when activities are available for use. Answers to the Workbook, Video Manual, and Lab Manual activities are located in a separate SAM Answer Key.

The Workbook

Each lesson's workbook activities focus on developing your reading and writing skills as they recycle the language of the corresponding textbook lesson. Exercise formats include, but are not limited to, true/false, multiple choice, fill-in-the-blanks, sentence completions, fleshing out sentences from key elements, and answering questions. You will also find activities based on drawings, photographs, and maps.

Reflecting the overall organization of the textbook lessons, each workbook lesson consists of **Contextos, Estructura,** and **Panorama** sections. After every three lessons, there is a **Repaso** section, providing cumulative practice of the grammar and vocabulary you learned over previous lessons.

The Video Manual
Fotonovela

The **VISTAS Fotonovela** video offers 6–9 minutes of footage for each of the textbook's lessons. Each episode tells the continuing story of a group of college students from various Spanish-speaking countries who are studying in Mexico. The video, shot in a variety of locations throughout Mexico, follows them through an academic year.

The video activities will guide you through the video episodes. **Antes de ver el video** offers previewing activities to prepare you for successful video viewing experiences. **Mientras ves el video** contains while-viewing activities. Lastly, **Después de ver el video** provides post-viewing questions that check your comprehension of the video. These are followed by some questions that ask you to apply what you have learned to your own life or offer your own opinions.

Panorama cultural

The **Panorama cultural** video is integrated with the **Panorama** section in each lesson of **VISTAS**. Each video is 2–3 minutes long and consists of documentary footage from the countries of focus. The images were specially chosen for interest level and visual appeal, while the all-Spanish narrations were carefully written to reflect the vocabulary and grammar covered in the text.

As you watch the videos, you will experience a diversity of images and topics: cities, monuments, traditions, festivals, archeological sites, geographical wonders, and more. You will be transported to each Spanish-speaking country, including the United States and Canada, thereby having the opportunity to expand your cultural perspectives with information directly related to the content of your textbook.

The video activities that accompany the **Panorama cultural** video will prepare you for viewing and guide you through the video modules using the same pre-, while-, and post-viewing activity structure as the **Fotonovela** video activities.

Flash cultura

The dynamic **Flash cultura** video is integrated with the **Adelante** section of each lesson. The video was filmed in eight countries. **Flash cultura**'s reporters take you on a tour of the sites and customs of the Spanish-speaking world. Along the way, they conduct impromptu interviews with the people they meet, who in turn share their own perspectives on their country and culture.

The segments will provide you with valuable cultural insights as well as authentic linguistic input as they gradually move into Spanish. Be prepared to listen to a wide variety of accents and vocabulary from the Spanish-speaking world!

Lab Manual

The Lab Manual activities are designed for use with the **VISTAS** Lab Audio Program MP3s on the Supersite (also available for purchase on CD). They focus on building your listening comprehension, speaking, and pronunciation skills in Spanish, as they reinforce the vocabulary and grammar of the corresponding textbook lesson. The Lab Manual guides you through the Lab Audio Program MP3 files, providing the written cues you will need in order to follow along easily. You will hear statements, questions, mini-dialogues, conversations, monologues, commercials, and many other kinds of listening passages, all recorded by native Spanish speakers. You will encounter a wide range of activities, such as listening-and-repeating exercises, listening-and-speaking practice, listening-and-writing activities, illustration-based work, and dictations.

Each lesson of the Lab Manual contains a **Contextos** section that practices the vocabulary taught in the corresponding textbook lesson. In **Lecciones 1–9**, a **Pronunciación** section follows; it parallels the one found in your textbook, and, in addition, offers a dictation exercise. In **Lecciones 10–18**, the **Pronunciación** sections are unique to the Lab Manual and the Lab MP3 files since, in those lessons, your textbook features **Ortografía** sections instead of **Pronunciación**. Each lesson then continues with an **Estructura** section and closes with a **Vocabulario** section that allows you to listen to and repeat the active vocabulary listed on the final page of the corresponding section in the student textbook.

We hope that you will find the **VISTAS 5/e** Student Activities Manual to be a useful language learning resource and that it will help you increase your Spanish language skills in a productive, enjoyable fashion.

*The **VISTAS 5/e** Authors and the Vista Higher Learning Editorial Staff*

Photography Credits

Workbook
22: (l) VHL; (m) © Elke Stolzenberg/Corbis; (r) José Blanco; **34:** (tl) Lauren Krolick; (bl) Martín Bernetti; (r) Ivan Mejia; **36:** Martín Bernetti; **38:** Martín Bernetti; **58:** (tl) © StockTrek/Photodisc/Getty Images; (tr) Carlos Gaudier; (bl) © Nanniqui/Dreamstime; (br) José Blanco; **72:** Ventus Pictures.

Lab Manual
15: Martín Bernetti.

contextos   Lección 1

1 **Saludos** For each question or expression, write the appropriate answer from the box in each blank.

| De nada. | Encantada. | Muy bien, gracias. | Nos vemos. |
| El gusto es mío. | Me llamo Pepe. | Nada. | Soy de Argentina. |

1. ¿Cómo te llamas? _____

2. ¿Qué hay de nuevo? _____

3. ¿De dónde eres? _____

4. Adiós. _____

5. ¿Cómo está usted? _____

6. Mucho gusto. _____

7. Te presento a la señora Díaz. _____

8. Muchas gracias. _____

2 **Conversación** Complete this conversation by writing one word in each blank.

ANA Buenos días, señor González. ¿Cómo (1)_____ (2)_____?

SR. GONZÁLEZ (3)_____ bien, gracias. ¿Y tú, (4)_____ estás?

ANA Regular. (5)_____ presento a Antonio.

SR. GONZÁLEZ Mucho (6)_____, Antonio.

ANTONIO El gusto (7)_____ (8)_____.

SR. GONZÁLEZ ¿De dónde (9)_____, Antonio?

ANTONIO (10)_____ (11)_____ México.

ANA (12)_____ luego, señor González.

SR. GONZÁLEZ Nos (13)_____, Ana.

ANTONIO (14)_____, señor González.

3 **Saludos, despedidas y presentaciones** Complete these phrases with the missing words. Then write each phrase in the correct column of the chart.

1. ¿_____ pasa?
2. _____ luego.
3. _____ gusto.
4. Te _____ a Irene.
5. ¿_____ estás?
6. _____ días.
7. El _____ es mío.
8. Nos _____.

Saludos	Despedidas	Presentaciones

© 2016 by Vista Higher Learning, Inc. All rights reserved.

Workbook

4   **Diferente** Write the word or phrase that does not belong in each group.

1. Hasta mañana.
   Nos vemos.
   Buenos días.
   Hasta pronto.

   _____

2. ¿Qué tal?
   Regular.
   ¿Qué pasa?
   ¿Cómo estás?

   _____

3. Igualmente.
   De nada.
   Mucho gusto.
   Encantada.

   _____

4. Muchas gracias.
   Muy bien, gracias.
   No muy bien.
   Regular.

   _____

5. ¿De dónde eres?
   ¿Cómo está usted?
   ¿De dónde es usted?
   ¿Cómo se llama usted?

   _____

6. Chau.
   Buenos días.
   Hola.
   ¿Qué tal?

   _____

   © 2016 by Vista Higher Learning, Inc. All rights reserved.

Workbook

estructura

1.1 Nouns and articles

1 **¿Masculino o femenino?** Write the correct definite article before each noun. Then write each article and noun in the correct column.

_____ hombre   _____ pasajero   _____ chico

_____ profesora   _____ mujer   _____ pasajera

_____ chica   _____ conductora   _____ profesor

Masculino	**Femenino**
_____	_____
_____	_____
_____	_____
_____	_____
_____	_____

2 **¿El, la, los o las?** Write the correct definite article before each noun.

1. _____ autobús   6. _____ mano
2. _____ maleta   7. _____ país
3. _____ lápices   8. _____ problema
4. _____ diccionario   9. _____ cosas
5. _____ palabras   10. _____ diarios

3 **Singular y plural** Give the plural form of each singular article and noun and the singular form of each plural article and noun.

1. unas fotografías _____   6. unas escuelas _____

2. un día _____   7. unos videos _____

3. un cuaderno _____   8. un programa _____

4. unos pasajeros _____   9. unos autobuses _____

5. una computadora _____   10. una palabra _____

4 **Las cosas** For each picture, provide the noun with its corresponding definite and indefinite articles.

1. _____   2. _____   3. _____   4. _____

Workbook

1.2 Numbers 0–30

1 **Los números** Solve the math problems to complete the crossword puzzle.

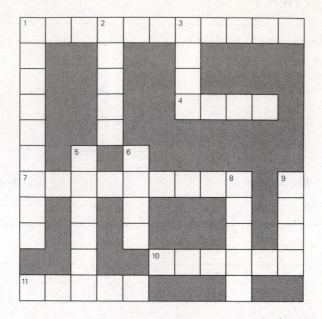

Horizontales

1. veinte más cinco
4. veintiséis menos quince
7. treinta menos catorce
10. veinticinco menos veintiuno
11. once más dos

Verticales

1. once más once
2. seis más tres
3. trece menos trece
5. doce más ocho

6. veintinueve menos diecinueve
8. veintitrés menos dieciséis
9. siete más uno

2 **¿Cuántos hay?** Write questions that ask how many items there are. Then write the answers. Write out the numbers.

> **modelo**
> 2 cuadernos
> ¿Cuántos cuadernos hay? Hay dos cuadernos.

1. 3 diccionarios _____

2. 12 estudiantes _____

3. 10 lápices _____

4. 7 maletas _____

5. 25 palabras _____

6. 21 países _____

7. 13 escuelas _____

8. 18 pasajeros _____

9. 15 computadoras _____

10. 27 fotografías _____

 © 2016 by Vista Higher Learning, Inc. All rights reserved.

1.3 Present tense of **ser**

1 **Los pronombres** In the second column, write the subject pronouns that you would use when addressing the people listed in the first column. In the third column, write the pronouns you would use when talking about them. The first item has been done for you.

Personas	Addressing them	Talking about them
1. el señor Díaz	usted	él
2. Jimena y Marissa		
3. Maru y Miguel		
4. la profesora		
5. un estudiante		
6. el director de una escuela		
7. tres chicas		
8. un pasajero de autobús		
9. Juan Carlos y Felipe		
10. una turista		

2 **Nosotros somos...** Rewrite each sentence with the new subject. Change the verb **ser** as necessary.

> modelo
> Ustedes son profesores.
> Nosotros *somos profesores.*

1. Nosotros somos estudiantes. Ustedes _____.

2. Usted es de Puerto Rico. Ella _____.

3. Nosotros somos conductores. Ellos _____.

4. Yo soy turista. Tú _____.

5. Ustedes son de México. Nosotras _____.

6. Ella es profesora. Yo _____.

7. Tú eres de España. Él _____.

8. Ellos son pasajeros. Ellas _____.

3 **¡Todos a bordo! (All aboard!)** Complete Jorge's introduction of his travelling companions with the correct forms of **ser**.

Hola, me llamo Jorge y (1)_____ de Cuba. Pilar y Nati (2)_____ de España. Pedro, Juan y Paco (3)_____ de México. Todos nosotros (4)_____ estudiantes. La señorita Blasco (5)_____ de San Antonio. Ella (6)_____ la profesora. Luis (7)_____ el conductor. Él (8)_____ de Puerto Rico. Ellos (9)_____ de los Estados Unidos. El autobús (10)_____ de la agencia Marazul. Todos nosotros (11)_____ pasajeros de la agencia de viajes Marazul. Perdón, ¿de dónde (12)_____ tú, quién (13)_____ ella y de quién (14)_____ las maletas?

© 2016 by Vista Higher Learning, Inc. All rights reserved.

Workbook

4 **¿De quién es?** Use **ser** + **de** (or **del**) to indicate that the object belongs to the person or people listed.

> **modelo**
> nombre / el pasajero
> **Es el nombre del pasajero.**

1. diccionario / el estudiante _____

2. cuadernos / las chicas _____

3. mano / Sara _____

4. maletas / la turista _____

5. computadoras / los profesores _____

6. autobús / el conductor _____

7. lápices / la joven _____

8. fotografía / los chicos _____

9. computadora / la directora _____

10. país / David _____

5 **¿De dónde son?** Use **ser** + **de** to indicate where the people are from.

> **modelo**
> Ustedes / Costa Rica
> **Ustedes son de Costa Rica.**

1. Lina y María / Colombia _____

2. El profesor / México _____

3. Tú y los jóvenes / Argentina _____

4. Las estudiantes / Estados Unidos _____

5. Ellos / Canadá _____

6. La mujer / Puerto Rico _____

7. Los turistas / España _____

8. Él y yo / Chile _____

9. Nosotras / Cuba _____

10. Usted / Venezuela _____

6 **¿De quién?** Write questions for these answers using the correct interrogative words from the list.

> **modelo**
> ¿De dónde son ellos?
> Ellos son de España.

cómo	dónde	de quién(es)	por qué
cuándo	de dónde	qué	quién(es)

1. _____
   Los lápices son de Alejandro.

2. _____
   Daniela es de Ecuador.

3. _____
   Es una foto.

4. _____
   Ellas son Claudia y Marta.

   © 2016 by Vista Higher Learning, Inc. All rights reserved.

Workbook

1.4 Telling time

1   **La hora**   Give the time shown on each clock using complete sentences.

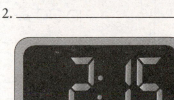

1. _____

2. _____

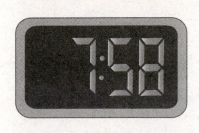

3. _____

4. _____

5. _____

6. _____

2   **¿Qué hora es?**   Use complete sentences to tell the time.

1. 3:40 p.m. _____

2. 6:00 a.m. _____

3. 9:15 p.m. _____

4. 12:00 a.m. _____

5. 1:10 p.m. _____

6. 10:45 a.m. _____

7. 5:05 p.m. _____

8. 11:50 p.m. _____

9. 1:30 a.m. _____

10. 10:00 p.m. _____

Workbook

3 **El día de Marta** Use the schedule to answer the questions in complete sentences.

8:45 a.m.	Biología
11:00 a.m.	Cálculo
12:00 p.m.	Almuerzo
2:00 p.m.	Literatura
4:15 p.m.	Yoga
10:30 p.m.	Programa especial

1. ¿A qué hora es la clase de biología? _____

2. ¿A qué hora es la clase de cálculo? _____

3. ¿A qué hora es el almuerzo (lunch)? _____

4. ¿A qué hora es la clase de literatura? _____

5. ¿A qué hora es la clase de yoga? _____

6. ¿A qué hora es el programa especial? _____

Síntesis

¿Y tú? Use lesson vocabulary, the present tense of **ser**, expressions for telling time, and numbers to answer the questions about yourself and your class using complete sentences.

1. ¿Cómo te llamas? _____

2. ¿De dónde eres? _____

3. ¿Qué hay de nuevo? _____

_____

4. ¿Qué hora es? _____

5. ¿A qué hora es la clase de español? _____

_____

6. ¿Cuántos estudiantes hay en la clase de español? _____

_____

7. ¿Hay estudiantes de México en la clase? _____

_____

8. ¿A qué hora es tu (your) programa de televisión favorito? _____

_____

© 2016 by Vista Higher Learning, Inc. All rights reserved.

panorama

Estados Unidos y Canadá

1 **¿Cierto o falso?** Indicate if each statement is **cierto** (*true*) or **falso** (*false*). Then correct the false statements.

1. La mayor parte de la población hispana de los Estados Unidos es de origen mexicano.

_____

2. Hay más (*more*) hispanos en Illinois que (*than*) en Texas.

_____

3. El estado con la mayor población hispana de los Estados Unidos es California.

_____

4. Muchos hispanos en Canadá tienen estudios universitarios.

_____

5. Muchos hispanos en Canadá hablan una de las lenguas oficiales: inglés o portugués.

_____

6. Hoy, uno de cada cuatro niños en los Estados Unidos es de origen hispano.

_____

7. Los tacos, las enchiladas y las quesadillas son platos cubanos.

_____

8. Las ciudades con más población hispana en Canadá son Montreal, Toronto y Vancouver.

_____

9. Un barrio cubanoamericano importante de Miami se llama la Pequeña Cuba.

_____

10. Los puertorriqueños de Nueva York celebran su origen con un desfile.

_____

2 **Completar** Complete the sentences with the correct information from **Panorama** about the Hispanic communities in Canada and the United States.

1. Se estima que en el año 2034 uno de cada tres _____ va a ser de origen hispano.

2. Los hispanos _____ activamente en la vida cotidiana y profesional de Canadá.

3. La Pequeña Habana es una _____ de Cuba en los Estados Unidos.

4. El desfile puertorriqueño es un gran espectáculo con carrozas y música _____,
_____ y hip-hop.

5. La comida mexicana es muy _____ en los Estados Unidos.

© 2016 by Vista Higher Learning, Inc. All rights reserved.   **Lección 1** Workbook Activities   **9**

3 **Un mapa** Write the name of each state numbered on the map and provide its Hispanic population (rounded to the nearest million).

Workbook

1. _____   (_____ millones de hispanos)

2. _____   (_____ millones de hispanos)

3. _____   (_____ millones de hispanos)

4. _____   (_____ millones de hispanos)

5. _____   (_____ millones de hispanos)

4 **¿De dónde es?** Write the origin of each item listed (**estadounidense, mexicano, cubano,** or **puertorriqueño**).

Origen

1. desfile en Nueva York   _____

2. enchiladas, tacos y quesadillas   _____

3. Pequeña Habana   _____

4. comida tex-mex y cali-mex   _____

5. mayor población hispana de EE.UU.   _____

  © 2016 by Vista Higher Learning, Inc. All rights reserved.

contextos

1 **Categorías** Read each group of items. Then write the word from the list that describes a category for the group.

| cafetería | clase | laboratorio |
| ciencias | geografía | materias |

1. sándwiches, tacos, sodas, bananas _____

2. mapas, capitales, países, nacionalidades _____

3. literatura, matemáticas, geografía, lenguas extranjeras _____

4. microscopios, experimentos, ciencias, elementos _____

5. física, química, biología, astronomía _____

6. pizarras, tiza, borrador, papelera, escritorios _____

2 **Buscar (To search)** Find school-related words in the grid, looking horizontally and vertically. Circle them in the puzzle, and write the words in the blanks with the correct accents.

S	P	F	Í	S	I	C	A	B	Q	G	Ñ	E
O	E	S	P	A	Ñ	O	L	E	U	S	B	R
C	X	B	E	C	O	N	O	M	Í	A	I	M
I	A	R	T	E	G	Q	F	A	M	F	O	I
O	M	C	A	C	L	O	U	R	I	V	L	N
L	E	P	R	U	E	B	A	A	C	D	O	G
O	N	U	E	O	N	E	Z	H	A	U	G	L
G	Ñ	D	A	M	C	L	A	S	E	T	Í	É
Í	E	J	I	L	C	I	E	N	C	I	A	S
A	P	E	R	I	O	D	I	S	M	O	P	I
D	S	T	H	O	R	A	R	I	O	Q	X	A
H	U	M	A	N	I	D	A	D	E	S	M	O

_____   _____

_____   _____

_____   _____

_____   _____

_____   _____

© 2016 by Vista Higher Learning, Inc. All rights reserved.

3 **El calendario** Use the calendar to answer these questions with complete sentences.

marzo

L	M	M	J	V	S	D
		1	2	3	4	5
6	7	8	9	10	11	12
13	14	15	16	17	18	19
20	21	22	23	24	25	26
27	28	29	30	31		

abril

L	M	M	J	V	S	D
					1	2
3	4	5	6	7	8	9
10	11	12	13	14	15	16
17	18	19	20	21	22	23
24	25	26	27	28	29	30

> **modelo**
> ¿Qué día de la semana es el 8 de abril (*April*)?
> El *8 de abril* es *sábado./Es sábado.*

1. ¿Qué día de la semana es el 21 de marzo (*March*)? _____

2. ¿Qué día de la semana es el 7 de abril? _____

3. ¿Qué día de la semana es el 2 de marzo? _____

4. ¿Qué día de la semana es el 28 de marzo? _____

5. ¿Qué día de la semana es el 19 de abril? _____

6. ¿Qué día de la semana es el 12 de marzo? _____

7. ¿Qué día de la semana es el 3 de abril? _____

8. ¿Qué día de la semana es el 22 de abril? _____

9. ¿Qué día de la semana es el 31 de marzo? _____

10. ¿Qué día de la semana es el 9 de abril? _____

4 **Completar** Complete these sentences using words from the word bank.

arte	ciencias	examen	horario	tarea
biblioteca	matemáticas	geografía	laboratorio	universidad

1. La biología, la química y la física son _____.

2. El _____ dice (*says*) a qué hora son las clases.

3. A las once hay un _____ de biología.

4. Martín es artista y toma (*takes*) una clase de _____.

5. Hay veinte calculadoras en la clase de _____.

6. Los experimentos se hacen (*are made*) en el _____.

7. Hay muchos libros en la _____.

8. Los mapas son importantes en el curso de _____.

     © 2016 by Vista Higher Learning, Inc. All rights reserved.

estructura

2.1 Present tense of -ar verbs

1 **Tabla (*Chart*) de verbos** Write the missing forms of each verb.

	Present tense				
Infinitivo	yo	tú	Ud., él, ella	nosotros/as	Uds., ellos
1. cantar					
2. _____	pregunto				
3. _____	_____	contestas			
4. _____			practica		
5. _____				deseamos	
6. _____					llevan

2 **Completar** Complete these sentences using the correct form of the verb in parentheses.

1. Los turistas _____ (viajar) en un autobús.

2. Elena y yo _____ (hablar) español en clase.

3. Los estudiantes _____ (llegar) a la residencia estudiantil.

4. Yo _____ (dibujar) un reloj en la pizarra.

5. La señora García _____ (comprar) libros en la librería de la universidad.

6. Francisco y tú _____ (regresar) de la biblioteca.

7. El semestre _____ (terminar) en mayo (*May*).

8. Tú _____ (buscar) a tus (*your*) compañeros de clase en la cafetería.

3 **¿Quién es?** Complete these sentences with the correct verb form so that the sentence makes sense.

busco	conversas	esperan	regresamos	trabaja
compran	enseña	necesitas	toman	viajan

1. Nosotras _____ a las seis de la tarde.

2. Muchos estudiantes _____ el curso de periodismo.

3. Rosa y Laura no _____ a Manuel.

4. Tú _____ con los chicos en la residencia estudiantil.

5. El compañero de cuarto de Jaime _____ en el laboratorio.

6. Yo _____ un libro en la biblioteca.

7. Rebeca y tú _____ unas maletas para viajar.

8. La profesora Reyes _____ el curso de español.

© 2016 by Vista Higher Learning, Inc. All rights reserved. **Lección 2** Workbook Activities **13**

Workbook

Workbook

4 **Usar los verbos** Form sentences using the words provided. Use the correct present tense or infinitive form of each verb.

1. una estudiante / desear / hablar / con su profesora de biología

_____

2. Mateo / desayunar / en la cafetería de la universidad

_____

3. (mí) / gustar / cantar y bailar

_____

4. los profesores / contestar / las preguntas (*questions*) de los estudiantes

_____

5. ¿(ti) / gustar / la clase de música?

_____

6. (nosotros) / esperar / viajar / a Madrid

_____

7. (yo) / necesitar / practicar / los verbos en español

_____

8. (mí) / no / gustar / los exámenes

_____

5 **¿Y tú?** Use complete sentences to answer these yes/no questions.

> modelo
> ¿Bailas el tango?
> Sí, bailo el tango./No, no bailo el tango.

1. ¿Estudias ciencias en la universidad?

_____

2. ¿Conversas mucho con los compañeros de clase?

_____

3. ¿Esperas estudiar administración de empresas?

_____

4. ¿Necesitas descansar después de (*after*) los exámenes?

_____

5. ¿Compras los libros en la librería?

_____

6. ¿Te gusta viajar?

_____

 © 2016 by Vista Higher Learning, Inc. All rights reserved.

2.2 Forming questions in Spanish

1 **Las preguntas** Make questions out of these statements by inverting the word order.

1. Ustedes son de Puerto Rico.

_____

2. El estudiante dibuja un mapa.

_____

3. Los turistas llegan en autobús.

_____

4. La clase termina a las dos de la tarde.

_____

5. Samuel trabaja en la biblioteca.

_____

6. Los chicos miran un programa.

_____

7. El profesor Miranda enseña la clase de humanidades.

_____

8. Isabel compra cinco libros de historia.

_____

9. Mariana y Javier preparan la tarea.

_____

10. Ellas conversan en la cafetería de la universidad.

_____

2 **Seleccionar** Choose an interrogative word from the list to write a question that corresponds with each response.

adónde	cuándo	de dónde	por qué	quién
cuáles	cuántos	dónde	qué	quiénes

1. _____

Ellos caminan a la biblioteca.

2. _____

El profesor de español es de México.

3. _____

Hay quince estudiantes en la clase.

4. _____

El compañero de cuarto de Jaime es Manuel.

5. _____

La clase de física es en el laboratorio.

6. _____

Julia lleva una computadora portátil.

7. _____

El programa de televisión termina en dos horas.

8. _____

Estudio biología porque hay un examen mañana.

Workbook

3

Muchas preguntas Form four different questions from each statement.

1. Mariana canta en el coro (*choir*) de la universidad.

_____

_____

_____

_____

2. Carlos busca el libro de arte.

_____

_____

_____

_____

3. La profesora Gutiérrez enseña contabilidad.

_____

_____

_____

_____

4. Ustedes necesitan hablar con el profesor de economía.

_____

_____

_____

_____

4

¿Qué palabra? Write the interrogative word or phrase that makes sense in each question.

1. ¿_____ es la clase de administración de empresas?
   Es en la biblioteca.

2. ¿_____ preparas la tarea de matemáticas?
   Preparo la tarea de matemáticas el lunes.

3. ¿_____ es el profesor de inglés?
   Es de los Estados Unidos.

4. ¿_____ libros hay en la clase de biología?
   Hay diez libros.

5. ¿_____ caminas con (*with*) Olga?
   Camino a la clase de biología con Olga.

6. ¿_____ enseña el profesor Hernández en la universidad?
   Enseña literatura.

7. ¿_____ llevas cinco libros en la mochila?
   Porque regreso de la biblioteca.

8. ¿_____ es la profesora de física?
   Es la señora Caballero.

   © 2016 by Vista Higher Learning, Inc. All rights reserved.

2.3 Present tense of estar

1   **Están en...** Answer the questions based on the pictures. Write complete sentences.

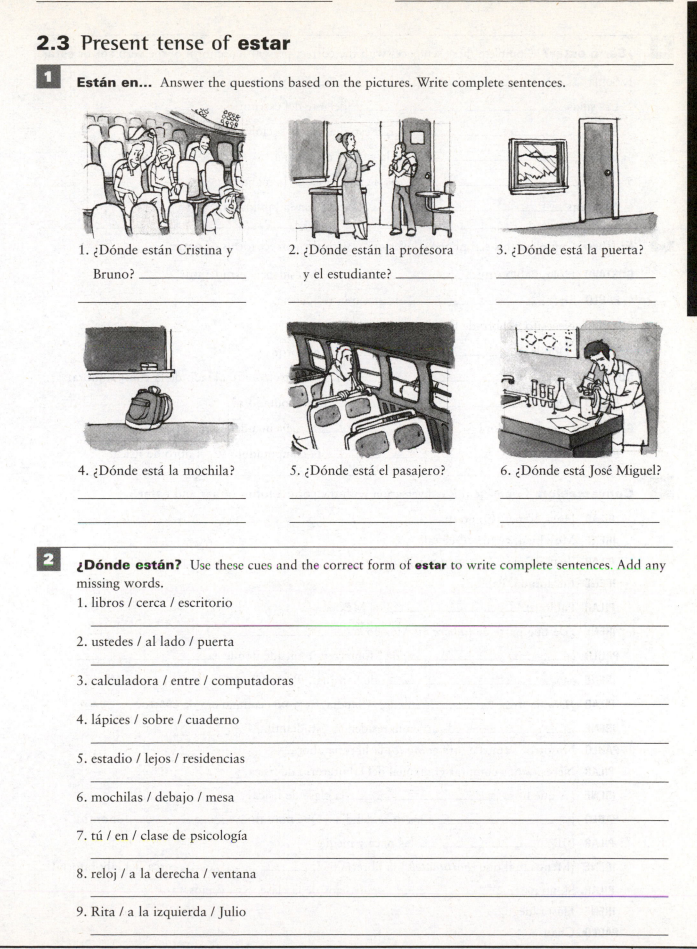

1. ¿Dónde están Cristina y Bruno? _____

2. ¿Dónde están la profesora y el estudiante? _____

3. ¿Dónde está la puerta? _____

4. ¿Dónde está la mochila? _____

5. ¿Dónde está el pasajero? _____

6. ¿Dónde está José Miguel? _____

2   **¿Dónde están?** Use these cues and the correct form of **estar** to write complete sentences. Add any missing words.

1. libros / cerca / escritorio

_____

2. ustedes / al lado / puerta

_____

3. calculadora / entre / computadoras

_____

4. lápices / sobre / cuaderno

_____

5. estadio / lejos / residencias

_____

6. mochilas / debajo / mesa

_____

7. tú / en / clase de psicología

_____

8. reloj / a la derecha / ventana

_____

9. Rita / a la izquierda / Julio

_____

3 **¿Ser o estar?** Complete these sentences with the correct present-tense form of the verb **ser** or **estar**.

1. Sonia _____ muy bien hoy.

2. Las sillas _____ delante del escritorio.

3. Ellos _____ estudiantes de sociología.

4. Alma _____ de la capital de España.

5. _____ las diez y media de la mañana.

6. Nosotras _____ en la biblioteca.

4 **El libro** Complete this cell phone conversation with the correct forms of **estar**.

GUSTAVO Hola, Pablo. ¿(1)_____ en la residencia estudiantil?

PABLO Sí, (2)_____ en la residencia.

GUSTAVO Necesito el libro de física.

PABLO ¿Dónde (3)_____ el libro?

GUSTAVO El libro (4)_____ en mi cuarto (*room*), al lado de la computadora.

PABLO ¿Dónde (5)_____ la computadora?

GUSTAVO La computadora (6)_____ encima del escritorio.

PABLO ¡Aquí (*Here*) (7)_____ la computadora y... el libro de física!

5 **Conversación** Complete this conversation with the correct forms of **ser** and **estar**.

PILAR Hola, Irene. ¿Cómo (1)_____?

IRENE Muy bien, ¿y tú? ¿Qué tal?

PILAR Bien, gracias. Te presento a Pablo.

IRENE Encantada, Pablo.

PILAR Pablo (2)_____ de México.

IRENE ¿De qué parte de (*where in*) México (3)_____?

PABLO (4)_____ de Monterrey. Y tú, ¿de dónde (5)_____?

IRENE (6)_____ de San Juan, Puerto Rico.

PILAR ¿Dónde (7)_____ Claudia, tu (*your*) compañera de cuarto?

IRENE (8)_____ en la residencia estudiantil.

PABLO Nosotros vamos a (*are going to*) la librería ahora.

PILAR Necesitamos comprar el manual del laboratorio de física.

IRENE ¿A qué hora (9)_____ la clase de física?

PABLO (10)_____ a las doce del día. ¿Qué hora (11)_____ ahora?

PILAR (12)_____ las once y media.

IRENE ¡Menos mal que (*Fortunately*) la librería (13)_____ cerca del laboratorio!

PILAR Sí, no (14)_____ muy lejos de la clase. Nos vemos.

IRENE Hasta luego.

PABLO Chau.

© 2016 by Vista Higher Learning, Inc. All rights reserved.

2.4 Numbers 31 and higher

1 **Números de teléfono** Provide the words for these telephone numbers.

modelo
968-3659
nueve, sesenta y ocho, treinta y seis, cincuenta y nueve

1. 776-7799

_____

2. 543-3162

_____

3. 483-4745

_____

4. 352-5073

_____

5. 888-7540

_____

6. 566-3857

_____

2 **¿Cuántos hay?** Use the inventory list to answer these questions about the amount of items in stock at the school bookstore. Use complete sentences and write out the Spanish words for numbers.

Inventario			
libros	320	mochilas	31
cuadernos	276	diccionarios	43
plumas	125	mapas	66

1. ¿Cuántos mapas hay? _____
2. ¿Cuántas mochilas hay? _____
3. ¿Cuántos diccionarios hay? _____
4. ¿Cuántos cuadernos hay? _____
5. ¿Cuántas plumas hay? _____
6. ¿Cuántos libros hay? _____

3 **Mi universidad** Use the information provided to complete the paragraph about your university. Write out the Spanish words for numbers.

25.000 estudiantes en total   44 nacionalidades diferentes   1.432 computadoras
350 españoles   10.500 libros   126 especialidades

Mi universidad es muy grande, hay (1)_____ estudiantes en el campus. Hay personas de (2)_____ países diferentes y (3)_____ son estudiantes de España. La biblioteca tiene (4)_____ libros de (5)_____ especialidades diferentes. Hay mucha tecnología; hay (6)_____ computadoras en el campus. ¡Me encanta mi universidad!

© 2016 by Vista Higher Learning, Inc. All rights reserved.

Workbook

4 **Por ciento** Use the pie chart to complete these sentences. Write out the Spanish numbers in words.

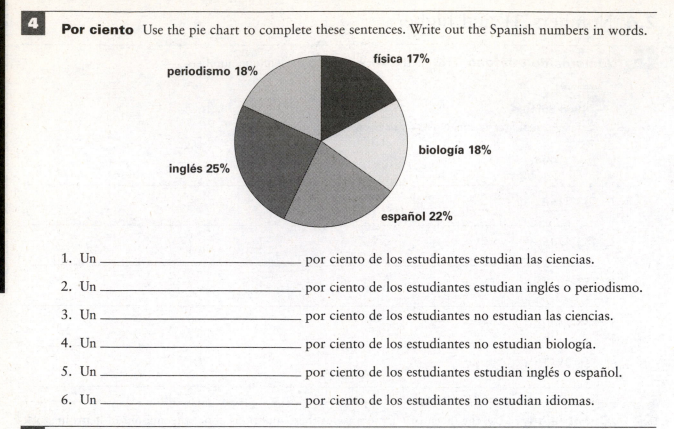

1. Un _____ por ciento de los estudiantes estudian las ciencias.

2. Un _____ por ciento de los estudiantes estudian inglés o periodismo.

3. Un _____ por ciento de los estudiantes no estudian las ciencias.

4. Un _____ por ciento de los estudiantes no estudian biología.

5. Un _____ por ciento de los estudiantes estudian inglés o español.

6. Un _____ por ciento de los estudiantes no estudian idiomas.

Síntesis

La universidad Imagine that a parent calls a college student during the second week of courses. Write questions that the parent might ask about the son or daughter's schedule, courses, and campus life. Use the cues provided. Then write possible answers. Use question words, the present tense of **estar**, the present tense of **-ar** verbs, and lesson vocabulary.

> **modelo**
> ¿A qué hora termina la clase de español?
> La clase de español termina a las tres.

- ¿A qué hora...?
- ¿Dónde está...?
- ¿Qué cursos...?
- ¿Trabajas...?
- ¿Estudias...?
- ¿Qué días de la semana...?
- ¿Hay...?
- ¿Cuántos...?

_____

_____

_____

_____

_____

_____

_____

    © 2016 by Vista Higher Learning, Inc. All rights reserved.

panorama

España

1 **¿De qué ciudad es?** Write the city or town in Spain associated with each item.

1. el Museo del Prado _____

2. el baile flamenco _____

3. la Sagrada Familia _____

4. La Tomatina _____

5. segunda (*second*) ciudad en población _____

2 **¿Cierto o falso?** Indicate whether each statement is **cierto** or **falso**. Then correct the false statements.

1. Las islas Canarias y las islas Baleares son de España.

_____

2. Zaragoza es una de las ciudades principales de España.

_____

3. La moneda de España es el peso.

_____

4. En España hay más de un idioma.

_____

5. La Tomatina es uno de los platos más deliciosos de España.

_____

6. El chef José Andrés vive en Washington, D.C.

_____

3 **El mapa de España** Fill in the blanks with the name of the city or geographical feature.

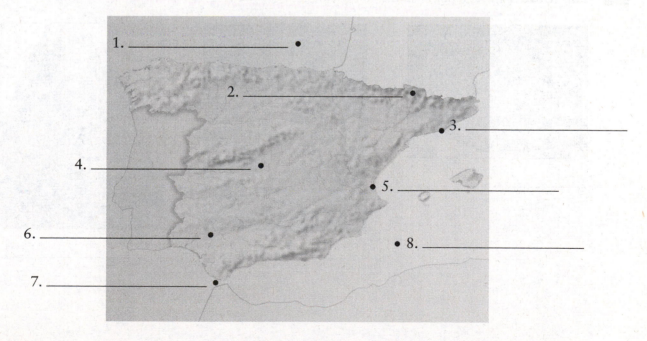

1. _____

2. _____

3. _____

4. _____

5. _____

6. _____

7. _____

8. _____

© 2016 by Vista Higher Learning, Inc. All rights reserved.   **Lección 2** Workbook Activities   **21**

4 **Profesiones** Complete these sentences with the person's occupation.

1. Fernando Alonso es _____.

2. Rosa Montero es _____.

3. Pedro Almodóvar es _____.

4. Miguel de Cervantes es _____.

5. Paz Vega es _____.

6. Diego Velázquez es _____.

5 **Palabras cruzadas (crossed)** Write one letter on each blank. Then answer the final question, using the new word that is formed.

1. Islas españolas del mar Mediterráneo

2. Español, catalán, gallego, valenciano y euskera

3. José Andrés es dueño (owner) de varios

4. Museo español famoso

5. Pintor español famoso

6. Obra más conocida de Diego Velázquez

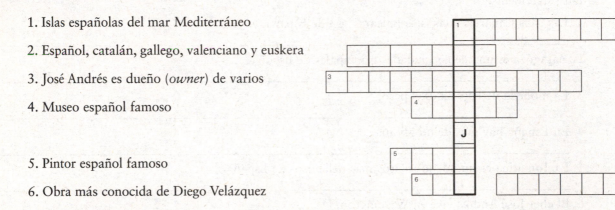

El aeropuerto (airport) de Madrid se llama _____.

6 **Las fotos** Label the object shown in each photo.

1. _____

2. _____

3. _____

© 2016 by Vista Higher Learning, Inc. All rights reserved.

contextos

1   **La familia** Look at the family tree and describe the relationships between these people.

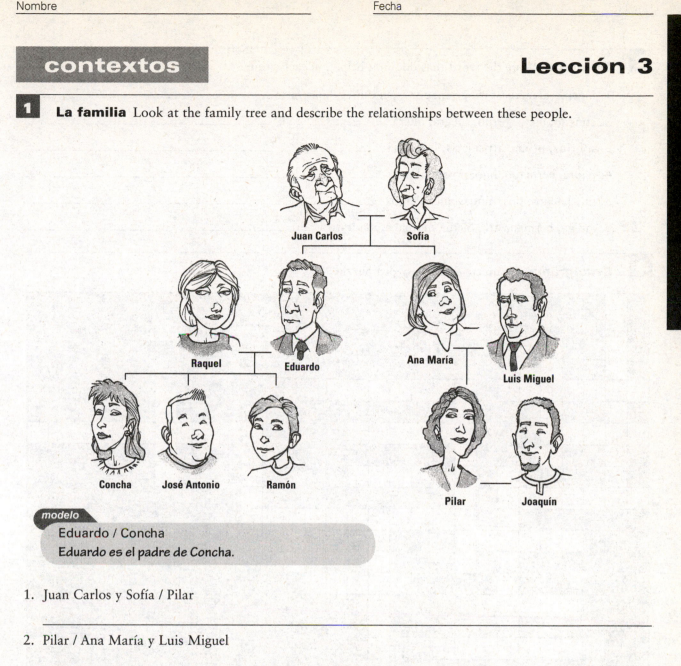

Juan Carlos   Sofía

Raquel   Eduardo   Ana María   Luis Miguel

Concha   José Antonio   Ramón   Pilar   Joaquín

> **modelo**
> Eduardo / Concha
> *Eduardo es el padre de Concha.*

1. Juan Carlos y Sofía / Pilar

   _____

2. Pilar / Ana María y Luis Miguel

   _____

3. Eduardo / Raquel

   _____

4. José Antonio y Ramón / Concha

   _____

5. Raquel / Pilar

   _____

6. Concha, José Antonio y Ramón / Pilar

   _____

7. Ana María / Raquel

   _____

8. Joaquín / Ana María y Luis Miguel

Workbook

2 **Diferente** Write the word that does not belong in each group.

1. ingeniera, médica, programadora, periodista, hijastra _____

2. cuñado, nieto, yerno, suegra, nuera _____

3. sobrina, prima, artista, tía, hermana _____

4. padre, hermano, hijo, novio, abuelo _____

5. muchachos, tíos, niños, chicos, hijos _____

6. amiga, hermanastra, media hermana, madrastra _____

3 **Crucigrama** Complete this crossword puzzle.

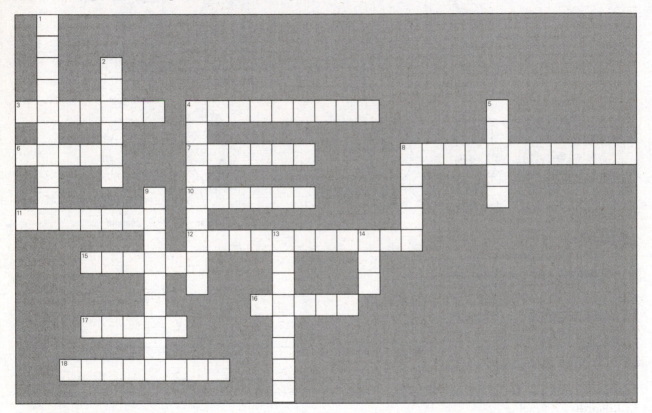

Horizontales

3. el hijo de mi hermano
4. la esposa de mi padre, pero no soy su hijo
6. el hijo de mi hija
7. el esposo de mi hermana
8. hombre que estudió (*studied*) computación
10. la madre de mi padre
11. padre, madre e (*and*) hijos
12. el hijo de mi madrastra, pero no de mi padre
15. doctor
16. tus nietos son los _____ de tus hijos
17. personas en general
18. la hija de mi esposa, pero no es mi hija

Verticales

1. mujer que escribe (*writes*) para el *New York Times*
2. compañeros inseparables
4. chicos
5. el esposo de mi madre es el _____ de mis abuelos
8. el hijo de mi tía
9. abuelos, primos, tíos, etc.
13. Pablo Picasso y Diego Velázquez
14. el hermano de mi madre

 © 2016 by Vista Higher Learning, Inc. All rights reserved.

estructura

3.1 Descriptive adjectives

1 **¿Cómo son?** Use the adjective in parentheses that agrees with each subject to write descriptive sentences about them.

> **modelo**
> **(gordo, delgada)**
> Lidia: Lidia *es delgada.*
> el novio de Olga: El *novio de Olga es gordo.*

(simpático, guapos, alta)

1. la profesora de historia: _____

2. David y Simón: _____

3. el artista: _____

(trabajadora, viejo, delgadas)

4. esas (*those*) muchachas: _____

5. el abuelo de Alberto: _____

6. la programadora: _____

2 **Descripciones** Complete each sentence with the correct form of the adjective in parentheses.

1. Lupe, Rosa y Tomás son _____ (bueno) amigos.

2. Ignacio es _____ (alto) y _____ (guapo).

3. Laura y Virginia son _____ (bajo) y _____ (delgado).

4. Pedro y Vanessa son _____ (moreno), pero Diana es _____ (pelirrojo).

5. Nosotras somos _____ (inteligente) y _____ (trabajador).

6. Esos (*Those*) chicos son _____ (simpático), pero son _____ (tonto).

3 **No** Answer these questions using the adjective with the opposite meaning.

> **modelo**
> ¿Es alta Manuela?
> No, *es baja.*

1. ¿Es antipático don Antonio? _____

2. ¿Son morenas las hermanas de Lupe? _____

3. ¿Es fea la mamá de Carlos? _____

4. ¿Son viejos los primos de Sofía? _____

5. ¿Son malos los padres de Alejandro? _____

6. ¿Es guapo el tío de Andrés? _____

© 2016 by Vista Higher Learning, Inc. All rights reserved.

Workbook

Workbook

4   **Origen y nacionalidad** Read the names and origins of the people in this tour group. Then write sentences saying what city they are from and what their nationalities are.

> modelo
> Álvaro Estrada / Miami, Estados Unidos
> Álvaro Estrada **es de Miami. Es estadounidense.**

1. Lucy y Lee Hung / Pekín, China _____

2. Pierre y Marie Lebrun / Montreal, Canadá _____

3. Luigi Mazzini / Roma, Italia _____

4. Elizabeth Mitchell / Londres, Inglaterra (*England*) _____

5. Roberto Morales / Madrid, España _____

6. Andrés y Patricia Padilla / La Habana, Cuba _____

7. Paula y Cecilia Robles / San José, Costa Rica _____

8. Arnold Schmidt / Berlín, Alemania (*Germany*) _____

9. Antoinette y Marie Valois / París, Francia _____

10. Marta Zedillo / Guadalajara, México _____

5   **Completar** Complete each sentence with the correct form of the adjective in parentheses.

(bueno)

1. La clase de matemáticas es muy _____.

2. Rogelio es un _____ compañero de cuarto.

3. Agustina compra una _____ mochila para (*for*) los libros.

4. Andrés y Guillermo son muy _____ estudiantes.

(malo)

5. Federico es antipático y una _____ persona.

6. Ahora es un _____ momento para descansar.

7. La comida (*food*) de la cafetería es _____.

8. Son unas semanas _____ para viajar.

(grande)

9. Hay un _____ evento en el estadio hoy.

10. Los problemas en esa (*that*) familia son muy _____.

11. La biblioteca de la universidad es _____.

12. La prima de Irma es una _____ amiga.

   © 2016 by Vista Higher Learning, Inc. All rights reserved.

3.2 Possessive adjectives

1 **¿De quién es?** Answer each question affirmatively using the correct possessive adjective.

> **modelo**
> ¿Es tu maleta?
> Sí, es mi maleta.

1. ¿Es la calculadora de Adela? _____

2. ¿Es mi clase de español? _____

3. ¿Son los papeles de la profesora? _____

4. ¿Es el diccionario de tu compañera de cuarto? _____

5. ¿Es tu novia? _____

6. ¿Son los lápices de ustedes? _____

2 **Familia** Write the appropriate forms of the possessive adjectives indicated in parentheses.

1. _____ (*My*) cuñada, Christine, es francesa.

2. _____ (*Their*) parientes están en Costa Rica.

3. ¿Quién es _____ (*your* fam.) tío?

4. _____ (*Our*) padres regresan a las diez.

5. Es _____ (*his*) tarea de matemáticas.

6. Linda y María son _____ (*my*) hijas.

7. ¿Dónde trabaja _____ (*your* form.) esposa?

8. _____ (*Our*) familia es grande.

3 **Clarificar** Add a prepositional phrase that clarifies to whom the item(s) belongs.

> **modelo**
> ¿Es su libro? (ellos)
> ¿Es el libro de ellos?

1. ¿Cuál es su problema? (ella)

_____

2. Trabajamos con su madre. (ellos)

_____

3. ¿Dónde están sus papeles? (ustedes)

_____

4. ¿Son sus plumas? (ella)

_____

5. ¿Quiénes son sus compañeros de cuarto? (él)

_____

6. ¿Cómo se llaman sus sobrinos? (usted)

_____

© 2016 by Vista Higher Learning, Inc. All rights reserved.

Workbook

Workbook

4 **Posesiones** Write sentences using possessive adjectives to indicate who owns these items.

> **modelo**
> Yo compro un escritorio.
> **Es mi** *escritorio.*

1. Ustedes compran cuatro sillas. _____

2. Tú compras una mochila. _____

3. Nosotros compramos una mesa. _____

4. Yo compro una maleta. _____

5. Él compra unos lápices. _____

6. Ellos compran una calculadora. _____

5 **Mi familia** Paula is talking about her family. Complete her description with the correct possessive adjectives.

Somos cinco hermanos. Ricardo, José Luis y Alejandro son (1)_____
hermanos. Francisco es (2)_____ cuñado. Es el esposo de (3)_____
hermana mayor, Mercedes. Francisco es argentino. (4)_____ papás viven en
Mar del Plata. Vicente es el hijo de (5)_____ hermano mayor, Ricardo. Él es
(6)_____ sobrino favorito. (7)_____ mamá se llama Isabel y es española.
Ellos viven con (8)_____ familia en Sevilla. José Luis estudia en Monterrey y vive
con la tía Remedios y (9)_____ dos hijos, Carlos y Raquel, (10)_____
primos. Alejandro y yo vivimos con (11)_____ papás en Guadalajara. Los papás
de (12)_____ mamá viven también con nosotros. Alejandro y yo compartimos
(13)_____ problemas con (14)_____ abuelos. Ellos son muy buenos.
Y tú, ¿cómo es (15)_____ familia?

6 **Preguntas** Answer these questions using possessive adjectives and the words in parentheses.

> **modelo**
> ¿Dónde está tu amiga? (Barcelona)
> **Mi amiga** *está en Barcelona.*

1. ¿Cómo es tu padre? (alto y moreno)

   _____

2. José, ¿dónde están mis papeles? (en el escritorio)

   _____

3. ¿Cómo es la escuela de Felipe? (pequeña y vieja)

   _____

4. ¿Son mexicanos los amigos de ustedes? (puertorriqueños)

   _____

5. Mami, ¿dónde está mi tarea? (en la mesa)

   _____

6. ¿Cómo son los hermanos de Pilar? (simpáticos)

   _____

   © 2016 by Vista Higher Learning, Inc. All rights reserved.

3.3 Present tense of **-er** and **-ir** verbs

1 **Conversaciones** Complete these conversations with the correct forms of the verbs in parentheses.

(leer)

1. —¿Qué _____, Ana?

2. —_____ un libro de historia.

(vivir)

3. —¿Dónde _____ ustedes?

4. —Nosotros _____ en Nueva York. ¿Y tú?

(comer)

5. —¿Qué _____ ustedes?

6. —Yo _____ un sándwich y Eduardo _____ pizza.

(deber)

7. —Profesora, ¿_____ abrir nuestros libros ahora?

8. —Sí, ustedes _____ abrir los libros en la página (*page*) 87.

(escribir)

9. —¿_____ un libro, Melinda?

10. —Sí, _____ un libro de ciencia ficción.

2 **Frases** Write complete sentences using the correct forms of the verbs in parentheses.

1. (nosotros) (Escribir) muchas composiciones en la clase de literatura.

_____

2. Esteban y Luisa (aprender) a bailar el tango.

_____

3. ¿Quién no (comprender) la lección de hoy?

_____

4. (tú) (Deber) comprar un mapa de Quito.

_____

5. Ellos no (recibir) muchos mensajes electrónicos (*e-mails*) de sus padres.

_____

6. (yo) (Buscar) unas fotos de mis primos.

_____

3 **¿Qué verbo es?** Choose the most logical verb to complete each sentence, and write the correct form.

1. Tú _____ (abrir, correr, decidir) en el parque (*park*), ¿no?

2. Yo _____ (asistir, compartir, leer) a conciertos de Juanes.

3. ¿_____ (aprender, creer, deber) a leer tu sobrino?

4. Yo no _____ (beber, vivir, comprender) la tarea de física.

5. Los estudiantes _____ (escribir, beber, comer) hamburguesas en la cafetería.

6. Mi esposo y yo _____ (decidir, leer, deber) el *Miami Herald*.

© 2016 by Vista Higher Learning, Inc. All rights reserved.   **Lección 3** Workbook Activities   **29**

Workbook

4   **Tú y ellos** Rewrite each sentence using the subject in parentheses. Change the verb form and possessive adjectives as needed.

> **modelo**
> Carolina no lee sus libros. (nosotros)
> *Nosotros no leemos nuestros libros.*

1. Rubén cree que la lección 3 es fácil. (ellos)

   _____

2. Mis hermanos aprenden alemán en la universidad. (mi tía)

   _____

3. Aprendemos a hablar, leer y escribir en la clase de español. (yo)

   _____

4. Sandra escribe en su diario todos los días (*every day*). (tú)

   _____

5. Comparto mis problemas con mis padres. (Víctor)

   _____

6. Vives en una residencia interesante y bonita. (nosotras)

   _____

5   **Descripciones** Look at the drawings and use these verbs to describe what the people are doing.

abrir   aprender   comer   leer

1. Nosotros _____   2. Yo _____

3. Mirta _____   4. Los estudiantes _____

© 2016 by Vista Higher Learning, Inc. All rights reserved.

Workbook

3.4 Present tense of **tener** and **venir**

1 **Completar** Complete these sentences with the correct forms of **tener** and **venir**.

1. ¿A qué hora _____ ustedes al estadio?

2. ¿_____ tú a la universidad en autobús?

3. Nosotros _____ una prueba de psicología mañana.

4. ¿Por qué no _____ Juan a la clase de literatura?

5. Yo _____ dos hermanos y mi prima _____ tres.

6. ¿_____ ustedes fotos de sus parientes?

7. Mis padres _____ unos amigos japoneses.

8. Inés _____ con su esposo y yo _____ con Ernesto.

9. Marta y yo no _____ al laboratorio los sábados.

10. ¿Cuántos nietos _____ tú?

11. Yo _____ una clase de contabilidad a las once de la mañana.

12. Mis amigos _____ a comer a la cafetería hoy.

2 **¿Qué tienen?** Rewrite each sentence, using the logical expression with **tener**.

1. Los estudiantes (tienen hambre, tienen miedo de) tomar el examen de química.

_____

2. Las turistas (tienen sueño, tienen prisa) por llegar al autobús.

_____

3. Mi madre (tiene cincuenta años, tiene razón) siempre (*always*).

_____

4. Vienes a la cafetería cuando (*when*) (tienes hambre, tienes frío).

_____

5. (Tengo razón, Tengo frío) en la biblioteca porque abren las ventanas.

_____

6. Rosaura y María (tienen calor, tienen ganas) de mirar la televisión.

_____

7. Nosotras (tenemos cuidado, no tenemos razón) con el sol (*sun*).

_____

8. David toma mucha agua cuando (*when*) (tiene miedo, tiene sed).

_____

3 **Expresiones con *tener*** Complete each sentence with the correct expression and the appropriate form of **tener**.

tener cuidado	tener miedo	tener mucha suerte	tener que
tener ganas	tener mucha hambre	tener prisa	tener razón

1. Mis sobrinos _____ del perro (*dog*) de mis abuelos.

2. Necesitas _____ con la computadora portátil (*laptop*).

3. Yo _____ practicar el vocabulario de español.

4. Lola y yo _____ de escuchar música latina.

5. Anita cree que (*that*) dos más dos son cinco. Ella no _____.

6. Ganas (*You win*) cien dólares en la lotería. Tú _____.

Síntesis

Tus parientes Choose an interesting relative of yours and write a description of that person. Use possessive adjectives, descriptive adjectives, the present tense of **tener** and **venir**, the present tense of **-er** and **-ir** verbs, and lesson vocabulary to answer these questions in your description.

- ¿Quién es?
- ¿Cómo es?
- ¿De dónde viene?
- ¿Cuántos hermanos/primos/hijos... tiene?
- ¿Cómo es su familia?
- ¿Dónde vive?
- ¿Cuántos años tiene?
- ¿De qué tiene miedo?

_____

_____

_____

_____

_____

_____

_____

_____

_____

_____

_____

_____

_____

© 2016 by Vista Higher Learning, Inc. All rights reserved.

panorama

Ecuador

1 **¿Cierto o falso?** Indicate whether the statements are **cierto** or **falso**. Correct the false statements.

1. Ecuador tiene aproximadamente el área de Rhode Island.

_____

2. Panamá y Chile limitan con (*border*) Ecuador.

_____

3. Las islas Galápagos están en el océano Pacífico.

_____

4. Quito está en la cordillera de los Andes.

_____

5. Todos (*All*) los ecuatorianos hablan lenguas indígenas.

_____

6. Rosalía Arteaga es novelista y pintora.

_____

7. Hay volcanes activos en Ecuador.

_____

8. Oswaldo Guayasamín fue un novelista ecuatoriano famoso.

_____

2 **El mapa de Ecuador** Fill in the blanks on this map with the correct geographical names.

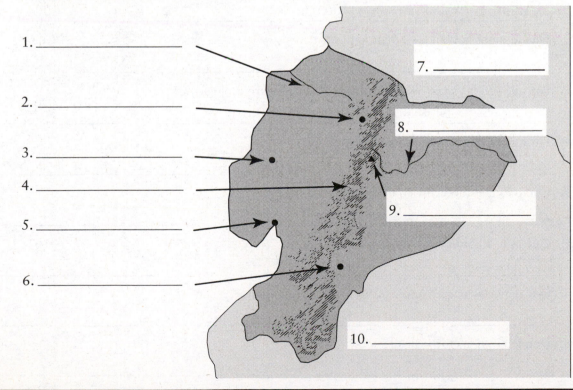

1. _____

2. _____

3. _____

4. _____

5. _____

6. _____

7. _____

8. _____

9. _____

10. _____

© 2016 by Vista Higher Learning, Inc. All rights reserved.   **Lección 3** Workbook Activities

Workbook

3   **Fotos de Ecuador** Label the place shown in each photograph.

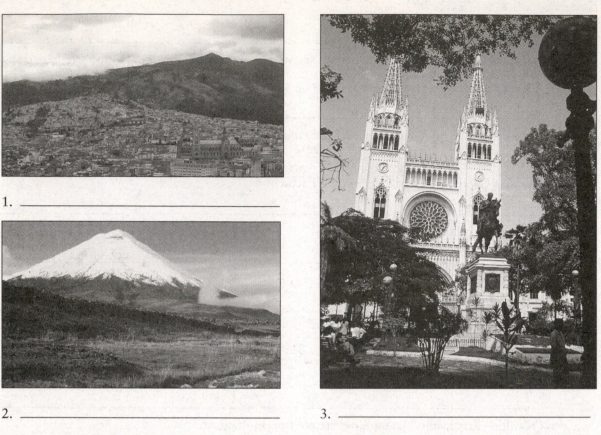

1. _____

2. _____

3. _____

4   **Descripción de Ecuador** Answer these questions using complete sentences.

1. ¿Cómo se llama la moneda de Ecuador?

_____

2. ¿Qué idiomas hablan los ecuatorianos?

_____

3. ¿Por qué son las islas Galápagos un verdadero tesoro ecológico?

_____

4. ¿Por qué vienen muchos turistas a Ecuador?

_____

5. ¿Cómo es el estilo artístico de Guayasamín?

_____

6. ¿Qué es la Mitad del Mundo?

_____

7. ¿Qué deportes puedes hacer (*can you do*) en los Andes?

_____

8. ¿Dónde viven las tortugas gigantes?

_____

© 2016 by Vista Higher Learning, Inc. All rights reserved.

repaso

Lecciones 1–3

1 **¿Ser o estar?** Complete each sentence with the correct form of **ser** or **estar**.

1. Los abuelos de Maricarmen _____ de España.

2. La cafetería de la universidad _____ cerca del estadio.

3. Gerónimo y Daniel _____ estudiantes de sociología.

4. —Hola, Gabriel. _____ María. ¿Cómo _____?

5. El cuaderno de español _____ debajo del libro de química.

6. Victoria no viene a clase hoy porque _____ enferma.

2 **¿Quiénes son?** Read the clues and complete the chart. Write out the numbers.

1. La persona de los Estados Unidos tiene 32 años.
2. David es de Canadá.
3. La programadora no es la persona de Cuba.
4. El conductor tiene 45 años.
5. Gloria es artista.
6. La médica tiene 51 años.
7. La persona de España tiene ocho años menos que el conductor.
8. Ana es programadora.

Nombre	Profesión	Edad (*Age*)	Nacionalidad
Raúl	estudiante	diecinueve	mexicano
Carmen			
			estadounidense
David			
	programadora		

3 **Oraciones** Form complete sentences using the words provided. Write out the words for numbers.

1. ¿cómo / estar / usted, / señora Rodríguez?

_____

2. estudiante / llegar / grande / biblioteca / 5:30 p.m.

_____

3. hay / 15 / cuadernos / sobre / escritorio

_____

4. nieto / Inés / aprender / español / escuela

_____

5. conductora / autobús / no / ser / antipático

_____

6. abuelo / Lisa / tener / 72 / años

_____

© 2016 by Vista Higher Learning, Inc. All rights reserved.

Workbook

4   Preguntas Write sentences with the words provided. Then make each statement into a question.

1. clase de contabilidad / ser / 11:45 a.m.

_____

_____

2. su tía / favorito / tener / 35 años

_____

_____

3. tu profesor / biología / ser / México

_____

_____

4. biblioteca / estar / cerca / residencia estudiantil

_____

_____

5   Los países Complete these sentences with information from the **Panorama** sections.

1. En Miami, hay un barrio cubano que se llama la _____.

2. Las personas de origen _____ son el grupo hispano más grande en los EE.UU.

3. Las islas Baleares y las islas Canarias son parte de _____.

4. La lengua indígena que más se habla en Ecuador es el _____.

6   Tu familia Imagine that these people are your relatives. Choose one and write several sentences about that person. First, say where the person is located in the photo. Include this information: name, relationship to you, profession, age, and place of origin. Describe the person and his or her activities using the adjectives and verbs you have learned.

_____

_____

_____

_____

contextos

1 Los deportes Name the sport associated with each object. Include the definite article.

1. _____   2. _____

3. _____   4. _____

5. _____   6. _____

2 Una es diferente Write the word that does not belong in each group.

1. pasatiempo, diversión, ratos libres, trabajar _____

2. patinar, descansar, esquiar, nadar, bucear _____

3. baloncesto, películas, fútbol, tenis, vóleibol _____

4. museo, equipo, jugador, partido, pelota _____

5. correo electrónico, revista, periódico, tenis _____

6. cine, deportivo, gimnasio, piscina, restaurante _____

3 **¿Qué son?** Write each of these words in the appropriate column in the chart.

andar en patineta	fútbol	montaña
baloncesto	gimnasio	natación
béisbol	jugar un videojuego	pasear
centro	leer una revista	restaurante

Deportes	Lugares	Actividades

4 **El fin de semana** Esteban is a very active young man. Complete the paragraph about his weekend with the appropriate words from the word bank.

Esteban

el centro	el monumento	una pelota
el cine	un museo	el periódico
deportes	la natación	la piscina
el gimnasio	el partido	un restaurante

Siempre leo (1)_____ los domingos por la mañana. Después, me gusta practicar

(2)_____. A veces, nado en (3)_____ que hay en el parque.

Cuando no nado, hago ejercicio (*exercise*) en (4)_____. Cuando hay mucho

tráfico en (5)_____, voy al gimnasio en bicicleta.

Cuando no como en casa, como en (6)_____ con mis amigos, y luego nosotros

podemos ver (7)_____ de béisbol. Algunos días, veo películas. Me gusta más ver

películas en (8)_____ que en mi casa.

 © 2016 by Vista Higher Learning, Inc. All rights reserved.

estructura

4.1 Present tense of **ir**

1 **Vamos a la universidad** Complete the paragraph with the correct forms of **ir**.

Alina, Cristina y yo somos buenas amigas. (Nosotras) (1)_____ a la universidad a las

ocho de la mañana todos los días (*every day*). Ellas y yo (2)_____ al centro de

computación y leemos el correo electrónico. A las nueve Alina y Cristina (3)_____

a su clase de psicología y yo (4)_____ a mi clase de historia. A las diez y media yo

(5)_____ a la biblioteca a estudiar. A las doce (yo) (6)_____ a

la cafetería y como con ellas. Luego (*Afterwards*), Alina y yo (7)_____ a

practicar deportes. Yo (8)_____ a practicar fútbol y Alina (9)_____

a la piscina. Cristina (10)_____ a trabajar en la librería. Los fines de semana Alina,

Cristina y yo (11)_____ al cine.

2 **Los planes** Mr. Díaz wants to make sure he knows about everything that is going on. Answer his questions in complete sentences using the words in parentheses.

1. ¿Adónde van Marissa y Felipe? (pasear por la ciudad)

_____

2. ¿Cuándo van a correr los chicos? (noche)

_____

3. ¿A qué hora van al Bosque de Chapultepec? (a las dos y media)

_____

4. ¿Cuándo van a ir a la playa? (martes)

_____

5. ¿Qué va a hacer Jimena en el parque? (leer un libro)

_____

6. ¿Qué va a hacer Felipe en el parque? (jugar al fútbol)

_____

Workbook

3 **Conversación** Complete this conversation with the correct forms of **ir**.

ELENA ¡Hola, Daniel! ¿Qué tal?

DANIEL Muy bien, gracias. ¿Y tú?

ELENA Muy bien. ¿Adónde (1)_____ ahora?

DANIEL (2)_____ al cine a ver una película. ¿Quieres (3)_____ conmigo?

ELENA No, gracias. Tengo mucha prisa ahora. (4)_____ al museo de arte.

DANIEL ¿Y adónde (5)_____ hoy por la noche?

ELENA Mi compañera de cuarto y yo (6)_____ a comer en un restaurante italiano. ¿Quieres (7)_____ con nosotras?

DANIEL ¡Sí! ¿Cómo (8)_____ ustedes al restaurante?

ELENA (9)_____ en autobús. Hay un autobús que (10)_____ directamente al barrio (*neighborhood*) italiano.

DANIEL ¿A qué hora (11)_____ ustedes?

ELENA Creo que (12)_____ a llegar al restaurante a las nueve.

DANIEL ¿Desean (13)_____ a bailar luego (*afterwards*)?

ELENA ¡Sí!

DANIEL (14)_____ a invitar a nuestro amigo Pablo también. ¡Nos vemos a las nueve!

ELENA ¡Chau, Daniel!

4 **¡Vamos!** Víctor is planning a weekend out with his friends. Combine elements from each column to describe what everyone is going to do. Use the correct verb forms.

ustedes	ver películas	el domingo
nosotros	ir al estadio de fútbol	el fin de semana
Víctor	tomar el sol	al mediodía
Claudio y su primo	visitar monumentos	a las tres
tú	pasear por el parque	por la noche
yo	comer en el restaurante	por la mañana

_____

_____

_____

_____

_____

_____

_____

_____

     © 2016 by Vista Higher Learning, Inc. All rights reserved.

4.2 Stem-changing verbs: e→ie, o→ue

1 **¿Qué hacen?** Write complete sentences using the cues provided.

1. Vicente y Francisco / jugar / al vóleibol los domingos

_____

2. Adela y yo / empezar / a tomar clases de tenis

_____

3. ustedes / volver / de Cancún el viernes

_____

4. los jugadores de béisbol / recordar / el partido importante

_____

5. la profesora / mostrar / las palabras del vocabulario

_____

6. Adán / preferir / escalar la montaña de noche

_____

7. (yo) / entender / el plan de estudios

_____

8. (tú) / cerrar / los libros y te vas a dormir

_____

2 **Quiero ir** Alejandro wants to go on a hike with his friends, but Gabriela says he doesn't have time. Write the correct forms of the verbs in parentheses.

ALEJANDRO ¿(1)_____ (poder) ir a la excursión con ustedes? Aunque (*Although*) tengo que volver a mi casa a las tres.

GABRIELA No, no (2)_____ (poder) venir. Nosotros (3)_____ (pensar) salir a las doce.

ALEJANDRO Yo (4)_____ (querer) ir. ¿(5)_____ (poder) ustedes volver a las dos?

GABRIELA No, tú tienes que comprender: Nosotros no (6)_____ (volver) a las dos. Nosotros (7)_____ (preferir) estar más tiempo en el pueblo.

ALEJANDRO Bueno, ¿a qué hora (8)_____ (pensar) regresar?

GABRIELA Yo no (9)_____ (pensar) volver hasta las nueve o las diez de la noche.

Workbook

3 **No, no quiero** Answer these questions negatively, using complete sentences.

> **modelo**
>
> ¿Puedes ir a la biblioteca a las once?
> No, no puedo ir a la biblioteca a las once.

1. ¿Quieren ustedes patinar en línea con nosotros?

   _____

2. ¿Recuerdan ellas los libros que necesitan?

   _____

3. ¿Prefieres jugar al fútbol a nadar en la piscina?

   _____

4. ¿Duermen tus sobrinos en casa de tu abuela?

   _____

5. ¿Juegan ustedes al baloncesto en la universidad?

   _____

6. ¿Piensas que la clase de química orgánica es difícil?

   _____

7. ¿Encuentras el programa de computadoras en la librería?

   _____

8. ¿Vuelven ustedes a casa los fines de semana?

   _____

9. ¿Puedo tomar el autobús a las once de la noche?

   _____

10. ¿Entendemos la tarea de psicología?

   _____

4 **Mensaje electrónico** Complete this e-mail message with the correct form of the logical verb. Use each verb once.

dormir
empezar
entender
jugar
pensar
poder
preferir
querer
volver

Para Daniel Moncada	De Paco	Asunto Saludo

Hola, Daniel. Estoy con Mario en la biblioteca. Los exámenes
(1)_____ mañana. Por las noches Mario y yo no (2)_____
mucho porque tenemos que estudiar. Tú (3)_____ cómo estamos,
¿no? Yo (4)_____ que los exámenes serán (*will be*) muy difíciles.
Tengo muchas ganas de volver al pueblo. Cuando (5)_____ al
pueblo puedo descansar. Yo (6)_____ el pueblo a la ciudad.
(7)_____ volver pronto.
Si (*If*) Mario y yo compramos pasajes (*tickets*) de autobús, (8)_____
pasar el fin de semana contigo. En casa (*At home*) mis hermanos y yo
(9)_____ al fútbol en nuestros ratos libres.

Nos vemos,
Paco

    © 2016 by Vista Higher Learning, Inc. All rights reserved.

4.3 Stem-changing verbs: e→i

1 **En el cine** Amalia and her brothers are going to the movies. Complete the story using the correct form of the verb provided.

1. Al entrar al cine, mis hermanos _____ (pedir) una soda.

2. Mis hermanos _____ (decir) que prefieren las películas de acción.

3. Nosotros _____ (pedir) ver la película de las seis y media.

4. Mis hermanos y yo _____ (conseguir) entradas (*tickets*) para estudiantes.

5. Yo _____ (repetir) el diálogo para mis hermanos.

6. Mis hermanos son pequeños y no _____ (seguir) bien la trama (*plot*) de la película.

2 **Conversaciones** Complete these conversations with the correct form of the verbs in parentheses.

(pedir)

1. —¿Qué _____ en la biblioteca, José?

2. — _____ un libro que necesito para el examen.

(conseguir)

3. —¿Dónde _____ ustedes las entradas (*tickets*) para los partidos de fútbol?

4. —Nosotros _____ las entradas en una oficina de la escuela.

(repetir)

5. —¿Quién _____ la excursión?

6. —Yo _____, me gusta mucho ese pueblo.

(seguir)

7. —¿Qué equipo _____ Manuel y Pedro?

8. —Pedro _____ a los Red Sox y Manuel _____ a los Yankees de Nueva York.

3 **¿Qué haces?** Imagine that you are writing in your diary. Choose at least five of these phrases and describe what you do on any given day. You should add any details you feel are necessary.

conseguir hablar español	pedir una pizza
conseguir el periódico	repetir una pregunta
pedir un libro	seguir las instrucciones

_____

_____

_____

_____

_____

© 2016 by Vista Higher Learning, Inc. All rights reserved.

Workbook

4 **La película** Read the paragraph. Then answer the questions using complete sentences.

Gastón y Lucía leen el periódico y deciden ir al cine. Un crítico dice que *Una noche en el centro* es buena. Ellos siguen la recomendación. Quieren conseguir entradas (*tickets*) para estudiantes, que son más baratas. Para conseguir entradas para estudiantes, deben ir a la oficina de la escuela antes de las seis de la tarde. La oficina cierra a las seis. Ellos corren para llegar a tiempo. Cuando ellos llegan, la oficina está cerrada y la secretaria está afuera (*outside*). Ellos le piden un favor a la secretaria. Explican que no tienen mucho dinero y necesitan entradas para estudiantes. La secretaria sonríe (*smiles*) y dice: "Está bien, pero es la última vez (*last time*)".

1. ¿Qué deciden hacer Gastón y Lucía?

_____

2. ¿Siguen la recomendación de quién?

_____

3. ¿Por qué Gastón y Lucía quieren conseguir entradas para estudiantes?

_____

4. ¿Cómo y cuándo pueden conseguir entradas para estudiantes?

_____

5. ¿Qué ocurre cuando llegan a la oficina de la escuela?

_____

_____

6. ¿Qué le piden a la secretaria? ¿Crees que ellos consiguen las entradas?

_____

_____

5 **Preguntas** Answer these questions, using complete sentences.

1. ¿Cómo consigues buenas calificaciones (*grades*)?

_____

2. ¿Dónde pides pizza?

_____

3. ¿Sigues a algún (*any*) equipo deportivo?

_____

4. ¿Qué dicen tus padres si no consigues buenas calificaciones?

_____

5. ¿Qué programas repiten en la televisión?

_____

 © 2016 by Vista Higher Learning, Inc. All rights reserved.

4.4 Verbs with irregular **yo** forms

1 **Hago muchas cosas** Complete each sentence by choosing the best verb and writing its correct form.

1. (Yo) _____ un disco de música latina. (oír, suponer, salir)

2. (Yo) _____ la hamburguesa y la soda sobre la mesa. (poner, oír, suponer)

3. (Yo) _____ la tarea porque hay un examen mañana. (salir, hacer, suponer)

4. (Yo) _____ a mi sobrina a mi clase de baile. (traer, salir, hacer)

5. (Yo) _____ una película sobre un gran equipo de béisbol. (salir, suponer, ver)

6. (Yo) _____ a bailar los jueves por la noche. (ver, salir, traer)

7. (Yo) _____ que la película es buena, pero no estoy seguro (*sure*). (hacer, poner, suponer)

8. (Yo) _____ mi computadora portátil (*laptop*) a clase en la mochila. (traer, salir, hacer)

2 **Completar** Complete these sentences with the correct verb. Use each verb in the **yo** form once.

hacer	suponer
oír	traer
salir	ver

1. _____ para la clase a las dos.

2. Los fines de semana _____ mi computadora a casa.

3. _____ que me gusta trabajar los sábados por la mañana.

4. Por las mañanas, _____ música en la radio.

5. Cuando tengo hambre, _____ un sándwich.

6. Para descansar, _____ películas en la televisión.

3 **Preguntas** Answer these questions, using complete sentences.

1. ¿Adónde sales a bailar con tus amigos?

_____

2. ¿Ves partidos de béisbol todos los fines de semana?

_____

3. ¿Oyes música clásica?

_____

4. ¿Traes una computadora portátil (*laptop*) a clase?

_____

5. ¿Cómo supones que va a ser el examen de español?

_____

6. ¿Cuándo sales a comer?

_____

© 2016 by Vista Higher Learning, Inc. All rights reserved. **Lección 4** Workbook Activities **45**

4 La descripción Read this description of Marisol. Then imagine that you are Marisol, and write a description of yourself based on the information you read. The first sentence has been done for you.

Marisol es estudiante de biología en la universidad. Hace sus tareas todas (*every*) las tardes y sale por las noches a bailar o a comer en un restaurante cerca de la universidad. Los fines de semana, Marisol va a su casa a descansar, pero (*but*) trae sus libros. En los ratos libres, oye música o ve una película en el cine. Si hay un partido de fútbol, Marisol pone la televisión y ve los partidos con su papá. Hace algo (*something*) de comer y pone la mesa (*sets the table*).

Soy estudiante de biología en la universidad. _____

_____

_____

_____

_____

_____

_____

_____

Síntesis

Interview a classmate about his or her pastimes, weekend activities, and favorite sports. Use these questions as guidelines, and prepare several more before the interview. Then, write up the interview in a question-and-answer format, faithfully reporting your classmate's responses. Use lesson vocabulary, stem-changing verbs, and the present tense of **ir**.

- ¿Cuáles son tus pasatiempos? ¿Dónde los practicas?
- ¿Cuál es tu deporte favorito? ¿Practicas ese (*that*) deporte? ¿Eres un(a) gran aficionado/a? ¿Tu equipo favorito pierde muchas veces? ¿Quién es tu jugador(a) favorito/a?
- ¿Adónde vas los fines de semana? ¿Qué piensas hacer este (*this*) viernes?
- ¿Duermes mucho los fines de semana? ¿Vuelves a casa muy tarde (*late*)?

_____

_____

_____

_____

_____

© 2016 by Vista Higher Learning, Inc. All rights reserved.

panorama

México

1 **Palabras** Use the clues to put the letters in order, spelling words in **Panorama**.

1. MGEÓINARIC _____
   resultado de la proximidad geográfica de México y los EE.UU.

2. ÍAD ED RMOTESU _____
   celebración en honor a las personas muertas

3. ALUJDAAAGRA _____
   ciudad número dos de México en población

4. ONETBI RZUEÁJ _____
   héroe nacional de México

5. CÁUNYAT _____
   península mexicana

6. ARSISTUT _____
   el D.F. atrae a miles de ellos

7. RADIF OKLAH _____
   la esposa de Diego Rivera

8. NGADORU _____
   estado mexicano que produce mucha plata

2 **¿Cierto o falso?** Indicate if each statement is **cierto** or **falso**. Then correct the false statements.

1. El área de México es casi dos veces el área de Texas.
   _____

2. Octavio Paz era un célebre periodista y narrador mexicano.
   _____

3. La geografía de México influye en aspectos económicos y sociales.
   _____

4. No hay mucho crecimiento en la población del D.F.
   _____

5. Frida Kahlo y Diego Rivera eran escritores.
   _____

6. El fin del imperio azteca comenzó (*started*) con la llegada (*arrival*) de los españoles en 1519.
   _____

7. Los turistas van a Guadalajara a ver las ruinas de Tenochtitlán.
   _____

8. México es el mayor productor de plata en el mundo.
   _____

© 2016 by Vista Higher Learning, Inc. All rights reserved. **Lección 4** Workbook Activities **47**

Workbook

Workbook

3

Completar Complete these sentences with the correct words.

1. México está localizado geográficamente al _____ de los Estados Unidos.

2. Hoy en día hay _____ de personas de ascendencia mexicana en los Estados Unidos.

3. Los idiomas que se hablan en México son el español, el _____ y _____.

4. Frida Kahlo, esposa del artista _____, es conocida por sus autorretratos (*self-portraits*).

5. El imperio _____ dominó México del siglo XIV al siglo XVI.

6. Se celebra el Día de Muertos en los _____.

4

¿Qué hacen? Write sentences using these cues and adding what you learned in **Panorama**.

1. la tercera (*third*) ciudad de México en población / ser

_____

2. la moneda mexicana / ser

_____

3. el Distrito Federal / atraer (*to attract*)

_____

4. muchos turistas / ir a ver las ruinas de

_____

5. el D.F. / tener una población mayor que las de

_____

6. tú / poder / ver / las obras de Diego Rivera y Frida Kahlo en

_____

5

Preguntas Answer these questions in complete sentences.

1. ¿Cuáles son las cinco ciudades más importantes de México?

_____

2. ¿Quiénes son seis mexicanos célebres?

_____

3. ¿Qué países hacen frontera (*border*) con México?

_____

4. ¿Cuál es un río importante de México?

_____

5. ¿Cuáles son dos sierras importantes de México?

_____

6. ¿Qué ciudad mexicana importante está en la frontera con los EE.UU.?

_____

7. ¿En qué siglo (*century*) fue (*was*) fundada la Ciudad de México?

_____

    © 2016 by Vista Higher Learning, Inc. All rights reserved.

contextos

1 **Viajes** Complete these sentences with the logical words.

1. Una persona que tiene una habitación en un hotel es _____.

2. El lugar donde los pasajeros esperan el tren es _____.

3. Para viajar en avión, tienes que ir _____.

4. Antes de entrar (*enter*) en el avión, tienes que mostrar _____.

5. La persona que trabaja en la recepción del hotel es _____.

6. Para planear (*plan*) tus vacaciones, puedes ir a _____.

7. El/la agente de viajes puede confirmar _____.

8. Para subir a tu habitación, tomas _____.

9. Para abrir la puerta de la habitación, necesitas _____.

10. Cuando una persona entra a otro país, tiene que mostrar _____.

2 **De vacaciones** Complete this conversation with the logical words.

aeropuerto	equipaje	llegada	playa
agente de viajes	habitación	pasajes	sacar fotos
cama	hotel	pasaportes	salida
confirmar	llave	pasear	taxi

ANTONIO ¿Llevas todo (*everything*) lo que vamos a necesitar para el viaje, Ana?

ANA Sí. Llevo los (1)_____ de avión. También llevo

los (2)_____ para entrar (*enter*) a Costa Rica.

ANTONIO Y yo tengo el (3)_____ con todas (*all*) nuestras cosas.

ANA ¿Tienes la cámara para (4)_____?

ANTONIO Sí, está en mi mochila.

ANA ¿Vamos al (5)_____ en metro?

ANTONIO No, vamos a llamar un (6)_____. Nos lleva directamente al aeropuerto.

ANA Voy a llamar al aeropuerto para (7)_____ la reservación.

ANTONIO La (8)_____ dice que está confirmada ya (*already*).

ANA Muy bien. Tengo muchas ganas de (9)_____ por Puntarenas.

ANTONIO Yo también. Quiero ir a la (10)_____ y nadar en el mar.

ANA ¿Cuál es la hora de (11)_____ al aeropuerto de San José?

ANTONIO Llegamos a las tres de la tarde y vamos directamente al (12)_____.

Workbook

3 **Los meses** Write the appropriate month next to each description or event.

1. el Día de San Valentín _____
2. el tercer mes del año _____
3. Hannukah _____

4. el Día de las Madres _____
5. el séptimo mes del año _____
6. el Día de Año Nuevo (*New*) _____

4 **Las estaciones** Answer these questions using complete sentences.

1. ¿Qué estación sigue al invierno? _____

2. ¿En qué estación va mucha gente a la playa? _____

3. ¿En qué estación empiezan las clases? _____

5 **El tiempo** Answer these questions with complete sentences based on the weather map.

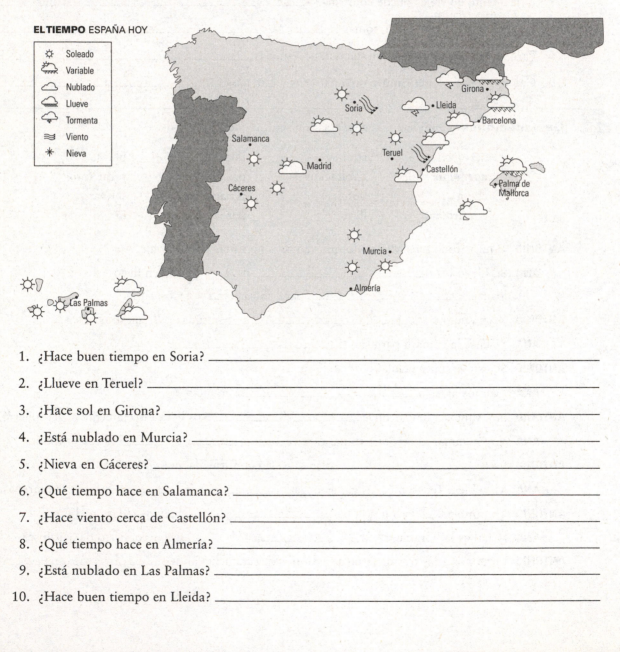

1. ¿Hace buen tiempo en Soria? _____

2. ¿Llueve en Teruel? _____

3. ¿Hace sol en Girona? _____

4. ¿Está nublado en Murcia? _____

5. ¿Nieva en Cáceres? _____

6. ¿Qué tiempo hace en Salamanca? _____

7. ¿Hace viento cerca de Castellón? _____

8. ¿Qué tiempo hace en Almería? _____

9. ¿Está nublado en Las Palmas? _____

10. ¿Hace buen tiempo en Lleida? _____

© 2016 by Vista Higher Learning, Inc. All rights reserved.

estructura

5.1 **Estar** with conditions and emotions

1 **¿Por qué?** Choose the best phrase to complete each sentence.

1. José Miguel está cansado porque...
   a. trabaja mucho.
   b. su familia lo quiere.
   c. quiere ir al cine.

2. Los viajeros están preocupados porque...
   a. es la hora de comer.
   b. va a pasar un huracán (*hurricane*).
   c. estudian matemáticas.

3. Maribel y Claudia están tristes porque...
   a. nieva mucho y no pueden salir.
   b. van a salir a bailar.
   c. sus amigos son simpáticos.

4. Los estudiantes están equivocados porque...
   a. estudian mucho.
   b. pasean en bicicleta.
   c. su respuesta es incorrecta.

5. Laura está enamorada porque...
   a. tiene que ir a la biblioteca.
   b. su novio es simpático, inteligente y guapo.
   c. sus amigas ven una película.

6. Mis abuelos están felices porque...
   a. vamos a pasar el verano con ellos.
   b. mucha gente toma el sol.
   c. el autobús no llega.

2 **Completar** Complete these sentences with the correct forms of **estar** and the conditions or emotions from the list.

abierto	cerrado	desordenado	sucio
aburrido	cómodo	equivocado	triste
cansado	contento	feliz	

1. No tenemos nada que hacer; _____ muy _____.

2. Humberto _____ muy _____ en su gran cama nueva (*new*).

3. Los estudiantes de filosofía no _____ _____; ellos tienen razón.

4. Cuando Estela llega a casa a las tres de la mañana, _____ muy _____.

5. La habitación _____ _____ porque no tengo tiempo (*time*) de organizar los libros y papeles.

6. Son las once de la noche; no puedo ir a la biblioteca ahora porque _____ _____.

7. El auto de mi tío _____ muy _____ por la nieve y el lodo (*mud*) de esta semana.

8. Mi papá canta en la casa cuando _____ _____.

9. Alberto _____ _____ porque sus amigos están muy lejos.

10. Las ventanas _____ _____ porque hace calor.

© 2016 by Vista Higher Learning, Inc. All rights reserved. **Lección 5** Workbook Activities **51**

3 **Marta y Juan** Complete this letter using **estar** + the correct forms of the emotions and conditions. Do not use terms more than once.

abierto	cómodo	enamorado	nervioso
aburrido	confundido	enojado	ocupado
avergonzado	contento	equivocado	seguro
cansado	desordenado	feliz	triste

Querida Marta:

¿Cómo estás? Yo (1)_____ porque mañana vuelvo a Puerto Rico y te voy a ver. Sé (I know) que tú (2)_____ porque tenemos que estar separados durante el semestre, pero (3)_____ de que (that) te van a aceptar en la universidad y que vas a venir en septiembre. La habitación en la residencia estudiantil no es grande, pero mi compañero de cuarto y yo (4)_____ aquí. Las ventanas son grandes y (5)_____ porque el tiempo es muy bueno en California. El cuarto no (6)_____ porque mi compañero de cuarto es muy ordenado. En la semana mis amigos y yo (7)_____ porque trabajamos y estudiamos muchas horas al día. Cuando llego a la residencia estudiantil por la noche, (8)_____ y me voy a dormir. Los fines de semana no (9)_____ porque hay muchas cosas que hacer en San Diego. Ahora (10)_____ porque mañana tengo que llegar al aeropuerto a las cinco de la mañana y está lejos de la universidad. Pero tengo ganas de estar contigo porque (11)_____ de ti (you) y (12)_____ porque te voy a ver mañana.

Te quiero mucho,

Juan

4 **¿Cómo están?** Read each sentence, then write a new one for each, using **estar** + an emotion or condition to tell how these people are doing or feeling.

> **modelo**
> Pepe tiene que trabajar muchas horas.
> *Pepe está ocupado.*

1. Vicente y Mónica tienen sueño. _____

2. No tenemos razón. _____

3. El pasajero tiene miedo. _____

4. Paloma se quiere casar con (marry) su novio. _____

5. Los abuelos de Irene van de vacaciones a Puerto Rico. _____

6. No sé (I don't know) si el examen va a ser fácil o difícil. _____

© 2016 by Vista Higher Learning, Inc. All rights reserved.

5.2 The present progressive

1   **Completar** Complete these sentences with the correct form of **estar** + the present participle of the verbs in parentheses.

1. Ana _____ (buscar) un apartamento en el centro de la ciudad.

2. Vamos a ver a mis primos que _____ (comer) en el café de la esquina.

3. (Yo) _____ (empezar) a entender muy bien el español.

4. Miguel y Elena _____ (vivir) en un apartamento en la playa.

5. El amigo de Antonio _____ (trabajar) en la oficina hoy.

6. (Tú) _____ (jugar) al *Monopolio* con tu sobrina y su amiga.

7. Las familias _____ (tener) muchos problemas con los hijos adolescentes.

8. El inspector de aduanas _____ (abrir) las maletas de Ramón.

9. (Nosotros) _____ (pensar) en ir de vacaciones a Costa Rica.

10. Mi compañera de cuarto _____ (estudiar) en la biblioteca esta tarde.

2   **Están haciendo muchas cosas** Look at the illustration and label what each person is doing. Use the present progressive.

1. El señor Rodríguez _____

_____ .

2. Pepe y Martita _____

_____ .

3. Paquito _____

_____ .

4. Kim _____

_____ .

5. Tus abuelos _____

_____ .

6. (Yo) _____

_____ .

7. La madre de David _____

_____ .

8. (Tú) _____

_____ .

Workbook

5.3 Ser and estar

1   Usos de *ser* y *estar* Complete these sentences with **ser** and **estar**. Then write the letter that corresponds to the correct use of the verb in the blank at the end of each sentence.

Uses of *ser*	**Uses of *estar***
a. Nationality and place of origin	i. Location or spatial relationships
b. Profession or occupation	j. Health
c. Characteristics of people and things	k. Physical states or conditions
d. Generalizations	l. Emotional states
e. Possession	m. Certain weather expressions
f. What something is made of	n. Ongoing actions (progressive tenses)
g. Time and date	
h. Where an event takes place	

1. El concierto de jazz _____ a las ocho de la noche. _____

2. Inés y Pancho _____ preocupados porque el examen va a ser difícil. _____

3. La playa _____ sucia porque hay muchos turistas. _____

4. No puedo salir a tomar el sol porque _____ nublado. _____

5. En el verano, Tito _____ empleado del hotel Brisas de Loíza. _____

6. Rita no puede venir al trabajo hoy porque _____ enferma. _____

7. La motocicleta nueva _____ de David. _____

8. (Yo) _____ estudiando en la biblioteca porque tengo un examen mañana. _____

9. La piscina del hotel _____ grande y bonita. _____

10. _____ importante estudiar, pero también tienes que descansar. _____

2   ¿Ser o estar? In each of the following pairs, complete one sentence with the correct form of **ser** and the other with the correct form of **estar**.

1. Irene todavía no _____ lista para salir.

   Ricardo _____ el chico más listo de la clase.

2. Tomás no es un buen amigo porque _____ muy aburrido.

   Quiero ir al cine porque _____ muy aburrida.

3. Mi mamá está en cama porque _____ mala del estómago (*stomach*).

   El restaurante chino que está cerca del laboratorio _____ muy malo.

4. La mochila de Javier _____ verde (*green*).

   No me gustan las bananas cuando _____ verdes.

5. Elena _____ más rubia por tomar el sol.

   La hija de mi profesor _____ rubia.

6. Gabriela _____ muy delgada porque está enferma (*sick*).

   Mi hermano _____ muy delgado.

   © 2016 by Vista Higher Learning, Inc. All rights reserved.

3 **En el hotel** Describe the Hotel San Juan using these cues and either **ser** or **estar** as appropriate.

1. la habitación / limpio y ordenado

_____

2. el restaurante del hotel / excelente

_____

3. la puerta del ascensor / abierta

_____

4. los otros huéspedes / franceses

_____

5. (yo) / cansada de viajar

_____

6. Paula y yo / buscando al botones

_____

7. la empleada / muy simpática

_____

8. el botones / ocupado

_____

9. ustedes / en la ciudad de San Juan

_____

10. (tú) / José Javier Fernández

_____

4 **La familia Piñero** Complete this paragraph with the correct forms of **ser** and **estar**.

Los Piñero (1)_____ de Nueva York, pero (2)_____ de vacaciones

en Puerto Rico. (3)_____ en un hotel grande en el pueblo de Dorado. Los padres

(4)_____ Elena y Manuel, y ahora (5)_____ comiendo en el

restaurante del hotel. Los hijos (6)_____ Cristina y Luis, y (7)_____

nadando en la piscina. Ahora mismo (8)_____ lloviendo, pero el sol va a salir

muy pronto (*soon*). Hoy (9)_____ lunes y la familia (10)_____

muy contenta porque puede descansar. El señor Piñero (11)_____ profesor

y la señora Piñero (12)_____ doctora. Los Piñero dicen: "¡Cuando

no (13)_____ de vacaciones, (14)_____ todo el tiempo

muy ocupados!".

© 2016 by Vista Higher Learning, Inc. All rights reserved.

Workbook

5.4 Direct object nouns and pronouns

1 **Monólogo de un viajero** Complete this monologue with the correct direct object pronouns.

Workbook

Hoy es lunes. El sábado voy de viaje. Tengo cinco días, ¿no? Sí, (1)_____ tengo. Tengo que conseguir un pasaje de ida y vuelta. ¡Imprescindible! Mi hermano trabaja en una agencia de viajes; él me (2)_____ consigue fácilmente. Tengo que buscar un buen mapa de la ciudad. En Internet (3)_____ puedo encontrar. Y en la biblioteca puedo encontrar libros sobre el país; libros sobre su historia, su arquitectura, su geografía, su gente... (4)_____ voy a leer en el avión. También quiero comprar una mochila nueva. Pero (5)_____ quiero muy grande. ¿Y dónde está mi vieja cámara de fotos? (6)_____ tengo que buscar esta noche. Voy a tomar muchas fotos; mi familia (7)_____ quiere ver. Y... ¿cuándo voy a hacer las maletas? (8)_____ tengo que hacer el miércoles. Y eso es todo, ¿verdad? No, no es todo. Necesito encontrar un compañero o una compañera de viaje. Pero, hay un pequeño problema: ¿dónde (9)_____ encuentro o (10)_____ encuentro?

Síntesis

On another sheet of paper, describe the room and the people in the illustration. Use complete sentences. Explain what the people are doing and feeling, and why. Then choose one of the groups of people and write a conversation that they could be having. They should discuss a vacation that they are planning, the arrangements they are making for it, and the things that they will need to take. Use **ser** and **estar**, the present progressive, **estar** with conditions and emotions, direct object nouns and pronouns, and lesson vocabulary.

 © 2016 by Vista Higher Learning, Inc. All rights reserved.

Workbook

panorama

Puerto Rico

1 **¿Cierto o falso?** Indicate if each statement is **cierto** or **falso**. Then correct the false statements.

1. El área de Puerto Rico es menor que (*smaller than*) la de Connecticut.

   _____

2. Todos (*All*) los puertorriqueños hablan inglés y español.

   _____

3. La fortaleza del Morro protegía (*protected*) la bahía de Mayagüez.

   _____

4. La música salsa tiene raíces españolas.

   _____

5. Los científicos detectan emisiones de radio desde (*from*) el Observatorio de Arecibo.

   _____

6. Los puertorriqueños no votan en las elecciones presidenciales de los Estados Unidos.

   _____

2 **Datos de Puerto Rico** Complete these sentences with words and expressions from **Panorama**.

1. Aproximadamente la mitad de la población de Puerto Rico vive en _____.
2. El uso del inglés es obligatorio en los documentos _____.
3. _____ fue (*was*) un beisbolista puertorriqueño famoso.
4. Hoy día _____ es el centro internacional de la salsa.
5. El Observatorio de Arecibo tiene uno de los _____ más grandes del mundo.
6. Puerto Rico se hizo parte de los EE.UU. en 1898 y se hizo un _____ en 1952.

3 **Cosas puertorriqueñas** Fill in each category with information from **Panorama**.

Ciudades puertorriqueñas	Ríos puertorriqueños	Islas puertorriqueñas	Puertorriqueños célebres

Workbook

4 **¿Lo hacen?** Answer these questions correctly using a direct object pronoun in each answer.

> **modelo**
> ¿Lees el artículo de Puerto Rico?
> *Sí, lo leo./ No, no lo leo.*

1. ¿Usan los pesos como moneda los puertorriqueños?

_____

2. ¿Habla el idioma inglés la cuarta parte de la población puertorriqueña?

_____

3. ¿Sacan fotografías del Morro muchas personas?

_____

4. ¿Tocan música salsa Felipe Rodríguez, El Gran Combo y Héctor Lavoe?

_____

5. ¿Estudian las montañas los científicos del Observatorio de Arecibo?

_____

6. ¿Pagan impuestos federales los puertorriqueños?

_____

5 **Fotos de Puerto Rico** Write the name of what is shown in each picture.

1. _____   2. _____

3. _____   4. _____

   © 2016 by Vista Higher Learning, Inc. All rights reserved.

Nombre _____ Fecha _____

contextos — Lección 6

1 El almacén Look at the department store directory. Then complete the sentences with terms from the word list.

Almacén Gema

PRIMER PISO	Departamento de caballeros
SEGUNDO PISO	Ropa de invierno y zapatos
TERCER PISO	Departamento de damas y óptica
CUARTO PISO	Ropa interior, ropa de verano y trajes de baño

abrigos · corbatas · sandalias
blusas · faldas · trajes de baño
bolsas · gafas de sol · trajes de hombre
botas · guantes · vestidos
calcetines · medias · zapatos de tenis
cinturones · pantalones de hombre

1. En el primer piso puedes encontrar _____
2. En el segundo piso puedes encontrar _____
3. En el tercer piso puedes encontrar _____
4. En el cuarto piso puedes encontrar _____
5. Quiero unos pantalones cortos. Voy al _____ piso.
6. Buscas unos lentes. Vas al _____ piso.
7. Arturo ve una chaqueta en el _____ piso.
8. Ana ve los jeans en el _____ piso.

2 Necesito muchas cosas Complete these sentences with the correct terms.

1. Voy a nadar en la piscina. Necesito _____.
2. Está lloviendo mucho. Necesito _____.
3. No puedo ver bien porque hace sol. Necesito _____.
4. Voy a correr por el parque. Necesito _____.
5. Queremos entrar en muchas tiendas diferentes. Vamos al _____.
6. No tengo dinero en la cartera. Voy a pagar con la _____.

© 2016 by Vista Higher Learning, Inc. All rights reserved.

Workbook

3   **Los colores** Answer these questions in complete sentences.

1. ¿De qué color es el chocolate?

_____

2. ¿De qué color son las bananas?

_____

3. ¿De qué color son las naranjas (*oranges*)?

_____

4. ¿De qué colores es la bandera (*flag*) de los Estados Unidos?

_____

5. ¿De qué color son las nubes (*clouds*) cuando está nublado?

_____

6. ¿De qué color son los bluejeans?

_____

7. ¿De qué color son muchos aviones?

_____

8. ¿De qué color son las palabras de este libro?

_____

4   **¿Qué lleva?** Look at the illustration and fill in the blanks with the names of the numbered items.

© 2016 by Vista Higher Learning, Inc. All rights reserved.

estructura

6.1 Saber and conocer

1 **¿Saber o conocer?** Complete the sentences, using **saber** and **conocer**.

1. (yo) No _____ a los padres de Juan Carlos.

2. Marissa _____ las ciudades de Canadá.

3. Maru, ¿(tú) _____ dónde estamos?

4. Yo _____ hablar italiano y francés.

5. La señora Díaz _____ bien la capital de México.

6. Jimena y yo no _____ a los otros turistas.

2 **¿Qué hacen?** Complete the sentences, using the verbs from the word bank. Use each verb only once.

conducir	ofrecer	saber
conocer	parecer	traducir

1. El señor Díaz _____ su automóvil todos los días.

2. Miguel _____ usar su computadora muy bien.

3. Jimena _____ ser una estudiante excelente.

4. Miguel y Maru no _____ bien al vendedor.

5. La Universidad del Mar _____ cursos muy interesantes.

6. Nosotros _____ libros a diferentes lenguas extranjeras.

3 **Oraciones completas** Create sentences, using the elements and **saber** or **conocer**.

1. Eugenia / mi amiga Frances

_____

2. Pamela / hablar español muy bien

_____

3. el sobrino de Rosa / leer y escribir

_____

4. José y Laura / la ciudad de Barcelona

_____

5. nosotros no / llegar a la residencia estudiantil

_____

6. yo / el profesor de literatura

_____

7. Elena y María Victoria / patinar en línea

_____

© 2016 by Vista Higher Learning, Inc. All rights reserved.   **Lección 6** Workbook Activities   **61**

Workbook

6.2 Indirect object pronouns

1 **¿A quién?** Complete these sentences with the correct indirect object pronouns.

1. _____ pido a la profesora los libros de español.

2. Amelia _____ pregunta a nosotras adónde queremos ir.

3. El empleado _____ busca trabajo a sus primas en el almacén.

4. Julio _____ quiere dar un televisor nuevo a sus padres.

5. Los clientes _____ piden rebajas a nosotros todos los años.

6. Tu hermano no _____ presta la ropa a ti (*you*).

7. La empleada de la tienda _____ cerró la puerta a mi tía.

8. La mamá no _____ hace la tarea a sus hijos.

9. _____ deben pagar mucho dinero a ti, porque llevas ropa muy cara.

10. Las dependientas _____ traen el vestido rosado a mí.

2 **Planes** Complete this paragraph with the correct indirect object pronouns and find out Sara's plans for this summer.

Mis amigos Loles, Antonio y Karen (1)_____ preguntan a mí si quiero ir a Italia con ellos

este verano. Yo (2)_____ digo: "¡Sí, síí, sííííí!" Ellos (3)_____ quieren pedir un libro

o dos a la profesora de historia del arte. Yo (4)_____ quiero dar a ellos un álbum de fotos

muy interesante. El novio de mi hermana es italiano. Él tiene una colección con dos mil cuatrocientas

sesenta y tres fotos de muchas ciudades y museos de su país. (5)_____ voy a preguntar a mi

hermana dónde lo tiene y a mis padres (6)_____ voy a decir: "¡Mamá, papá, en agosto voy

a Italia con unos amigos! La señorita Casanova (7)_____ va a prestar un par de libros y el

novio de Ángeles (8)_____ va a prestar su maravilloso álbum de fotos".

Loles tiene suerte. Su tía (9)_____ va a pagar el pasaje. Antonio y Karen van a trabajar en el

centro comercial los meses de junio y julio. ¿Y yo qué hago? ¿Quién (10)_____ va a pagar

el pasaje a mí? ¿A quién (11)_____ pido dinero yo? ¿A papá?... Pero él (12)_____

dice: "Sarita, hija, lo siento, pero yo no (13)_____ puedo pagar tu pasaje. Tu prima

(14)_____ puede dar trabajo de dependienta en su tienda de ropa". ¡¡¿Trabajo?!!

© 2016 by Vista Higher Learning, Inc. All rights reserved.

3 **Delante o detrás** Rewrite these sentences, using an alternate placement for the indirect object pronouns.

> **modelo**
> Me quiero comprar un coche nuevo.
> *Quiero comprarme un coche nuevo.*

1. Les vas a dar muchos regalos a tus padres.

_____

2. Quiero comprarles unos guantes a mis sobrinos.

_____

3. Clara va a venderle sus libros de literatura francesa a su amiga.

_____

4. Los clientes nos pueden pagar con tarjeta de crédito.

_____

4 **De compras** Complete the paragraph with the correct indirect object pronouns.

Isabel y yo vamos de compras al centro comercial. Yo (1)_____ tengo que comprar unas cosas a mis parientes porque voy a viajar a mi ciudad este fin de semana. A mi hermana Laura (2)_____ quiero comprar unas gafas de sol, pero ella (3)_____ tiene que comprar un traje de baño a mí. A mis dos sobrinos (4)_____ voy a comprar una pelota de béisbol. A mi padre (5)_____ llevo un libro y a mi madre (6)_____ tengo que conseguir una blusa. (7)_____ quiero llevar camisetas con el nombre de mi universidad a todos.

5 **Respuestas** Answer these questions negatively. Use indirect object pronouns in the answer.

> **modelo**
> ¿Le compras una camisa a tu novio?
> *No, no le compro una camisa.*

1. ¿Le escribe Rolando un mensaje electrónico a Miguel?

_____

2. ¿Nos trae el botones las maletas a la habitación?

_____

3. ¿Les dan gafas de sol los vendedores a los turistas?

_____

4. ¿Te compra botas en el invierno tu mamá?

_____

5. ¿Les muestra el traje a ustedes el dependiente?

_____

6. ¿Me vas a buscar la revista en la librería?

_____

© 2016 by Vista Higher Learning, Inc. All rights reserved.

Workbook

6.3 Preterite tense of regular verbs

1 **El pretérito** Complete these sentences with the preterite tense of the indicated verb.

1. Marcela _____ (encontrar) las sandalias debajo de la cama.

2. Gustavo _____ (recibir) un regalo muy bonito.

3. Sara y Viviana _____ (terminar) el libro al mismo tiempo.

4. La agente de viajes _____ (preparar) un itinerario muy interesante.

5. (yo) _____ (visitar) la ciudad en invierno.

6. Los dependientes _____ (escuchar) el partido por la radio.

7. Patricia y tú _____ (viajar) a México el verano pasado.

8. (nosotras) _____ (escribir) una carta al empleado del almacén.

9. (tú) _____ (regresar) del centro comercial a las cinco de la tarde.

10. Ustedes _____ (vivir) en casa de sus padres.

2 **Ahora y en el pasado** Rewrite these sentences in the preterite tense.

1. Ramón escribe una carta al director del programa.

2. Mi tía trabaja de dependienta en un gran almacén.

3. Comprendo el trabajo de la clase de biología.

4. La familia de Daniel vive en Argentina.

5. Virginia y sus amigos comen en el café de la librería.

6. Los ingenieros terminan la construcción de la tienda en junio.

7. Cada día llevas ropa muy elegante.

8. Los turistas caminan, compran y descansan.

9. Corremos cada día en el parque.

© 2016 by Vista Higher Learning, Inc. All rights reserved.

3 **Confundido** Your friend Mario has a terrible memory. Answer his questions negatively, indicating that what he asks already happened.

> **modelo**
> ¿Va a comprar ropa Silvia en el centro comercial?
> No, Silvia ya *compró ropa en el centro comercial.*

1. ¿Va a viajar a Perú tu primo Andrés?

_____

2. ¿Vas a buscar una tienda de computadoras en el centro comercial?

_____

3. ¿Vamos a encontrar muchas rebajas en el centro?

_____

4. ¿Va María a pagar las sandalias en la caja?

_____

5. ¿Van a regatear con el vendedor Mónica y Carlos?

_____

6. ¿Va a pasear por la playa tu abuela?

_____

4 **La semana pasada** Now Mario wants to know what you did last week. Write his question, then answer it affirmatively or negatively.

> **modelo**
> sacar fotos de los amigos
> —¿Sacaste fotos de los amigos?
> —Sí, saqué fotos de los amigos./No, no saqué fotos de los amigos.

1. pagar el abrigo con la tarjeta de crédito

_____

_____

2. jugar al tenis

_____

_____

3. buscar un libro en la biblioteca

_____

_____

4. llegar tarde a clase

_____

_____

5. empezar a escribir una carta

_____

_____

© 2016 by Vista Higher Learning, Inc. All rights reserved.

Workbook

Workbook

6.4 Demonstrative adjectives and pronouns

1 **De compras** Complete these sentences with the correct form of the adjective in parentheses.

1. Me quiero comprar _____ (*these*) zapatos porque me gustan mucho.

2. Comimos en _____ (*that*) centro comercial la semana pasada.

3. _____ (*that over there*) tienda vende las gafas de sol a un precio muy alto.

4. Las rebajas en _____ (*this*) almacén son legendarias.

5. _____ (*those*) botas hacen juego con tus pantalones negros.

6. Voy a llevar _____ (*these*) pantalones con la blusa roja.

2 **Claro que no** Your friend Mario hates shopping, and can't keep anything straight. Answer his questions negatively, using the cues in parentheses and the corresponding demonstrative adjectives.

> **modelo**
> ¿Compró esas medias Sonia? (cartera)
> No, compró esa cartera.

1. ¿Va a comprar ese suéter Gloria? (pantalones)

_____

2. ¿Llevaste estas sandalias? (zapatos de tenis)

_____

3. ¿Quieres ver esta ropa interior? (medias)

_____

4. ¿Usa aquel traje David? (chaqueta negra)

_____

5. ¿Decidió Silvia comprar esas gafas de sol? (sombrero)

_____

6. ¿Te mostró el vestido aquella vendedora? (dependiente)

_____

3 **Ésos no** Complete these sentences using demonstrative pronouns. Choose a pronoun for each sentence, paying attention to agreement.

1. Aquellas sandalias son muy cómodas, pero _____ son más elegantes.

2. Esos vestidos largos son muy caros; voy a comprar _____.

3. No puedo usar esta tarjeta de crédito; tengo que usar _____.

4. Esos zapatos tienen buen precio, pero _____ no.

5. Prefiero este sombrero porque _____ es muy grande.

6. Estas medias son buenas; las prefiero a _____.

    © 2016 by Vista Higher Learning, Inc. All rights reserved.

4 **Éstas y aquéllas** Look at the illustration and complete this conversation with the appropriate demonstrative adjectives and pronouns. Use the correct forms of **este**, **ese**, and **aquel**.

CLAUDIA ¿Quieres comprar (1)_____ corbata, Gerardo?

GERARDO No, no quiero comprar (2)_____. Prefiero (3)_____ del escaparate (*display case*).

CLAUDIA (4)_____ es bonita, pero no hace juego con tu chaqueta.

GERARDO Mira (5)_____ chaqueta. Es muy elegante y está a buen precio. Sí, puedo usar (6)_____ y darle a mi hermano ésta.

CLAUDIA ¿Y (7)_____ cinturón?

GERARDO (8)_____ es muy elegante. ¿Es caro?

CLAUDIA Es más barato que (9)_____ tres del escaparate.

5 **Más compras** Pilar and Marta are at the mall trying to get a new outfit for a special occasion. Write the conversation in which they talk about different clothing. Use at least six expressions from the list.

aquel vendedor	esa camisa	esos colores	esta falda
aquellas botas	ese precio	esos zapatos	este vestido

_____

_____

_____

_____

_____

_____

_____

Workbook

Síntesis

Imagine that you went with your brother to an open-air market last weekend. This weekend you take a friend there. Write a conversation between you and your friend, using as many different verbs as you can from those you have learned.

• Indicate to your friend the items you saw last weekend, what you liked and didn't like, the items that you bought, how much you paid for them, and for whom you bought the items.

• Suggest items that your friend might buy and for whom he or she might buy them. Use the preterite tense of regular verbs, indirect object pronouns, and lesson vocabulary.

_____

_____

_____

_____

_____

_____

_____

_____

_____

_____

_____

_____

_____

_____

_____

_____

_____

_____

_____

_____

_____

_____

_____

_____

 © 2016 by Vista Higher Learning, Inc. All rights reserved.

Workbook

 panorama

Cuba

1 **Crucigrama (Crossword)** Complete this crossword puzzle with the correct terms.

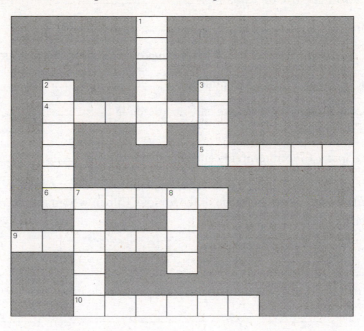

Horizontales

4. Nombre de la bailarina que fundó el Ballet Nacional de Cuba
5. Especie cubana de colibrí
6. Calle de la Habana Vieja frecuentada por Hemingway
9. Apellido de una escritora cubana célebre
10. Uno de los productos agrícolas más importantes en Cuba

Verticales

1. Esta organización declaró a la Habana Vieja Patrimonio Cultural de la Humanidad.
2. Apellido del ex líder del gobierno de Cuba
3. El azúcar se saca (is extracted) de esta planta.
7. Alicia Alonso practicaba (practiced) este baile.
8. Moneda cubana

2 **Preguntas de Cuba** Answer these questions about Cuba in complete sentences.

1. ¿De dónde son los antepasados de muchos cubanos de hoy en día?

_____

2. ¿De qué colores es la bandera cubana?

_____

3. ¿Cuál es un medio de transporte muy popular en Cuba?

_____

4. ¿Qué es *Buena Vista Social Club*?

_____

3 **Datos de Cuba** Complete these sentences with information from **Panorama**.

1. El _____ en la Plaza de Armas de la Habana Vieja es ahora un museo.

2. En Cuba se encuentran la Cordillera de los _____ y la Sierra _____.

3. Una isla que forma parte de Cuba es la _____.

4. Alicia Alonso fundó el _____ en 1948.

5. La _____ es un producto de exportación muy importante para Cuba.

6. El tabaco se usa para fabricar los famosos _____.

7. La inmigración fue muy importante en Cuba desde la _____ hasta mediados del siglo XX.

8. *Buena Vista Social Club* interpreta canciones clásicas del _____.

4 **Cubanos célebres** Write the name of the famous Cuban who might have said each of these quotations.

1. "Nací en 1927 y mi música es famosa."

_____

2. "Me convertí en una estrella internacional con el Ballet de Nueva York en 1943."

_____

3. "Soy el ex jefe de las fuerzas armadas de Cuba."

_____

4. "Viví en el siglo (*century*) diecinueve y escribí poemas."

_____

5. "Tengo más de cincuenta años, soy cubana y escribo libros."

_____

6. "Curé a muchas personas enfermas y estudié las ciencias."

_____

5 **Números cubanos** Write out the numbers in Spanish that complete these sentences about Cuba.

1. Hay _____ habitantes en la isla de Cuba.

2. Hay _____ habitantes en La Habana.

3. En el año _____ la Habana Vieja fue declarada Patrimonio Cultural de la Humanidad.

4. El área de Cuba es de _____ millas cuadradas.

5. El colibrí abeja de Cuba es una de las más de _____ especies de colibrí del mundo.

6. En el año _____ nació Fidel Castro.

   © 2016 by Vista Higher Learning, Inc. All rights reserved.

repaso   **Lecciones 4–6**

Workbook

1 **No lo hago** Answer these questions affirmatively or negatively as indicated, replacing the direct object with a direct object pronoun.

> **modelo**
>
> ¿Traes la computadora a clase? (no)
> No, no la traigo.

1. ¿Haces la tarea de economía en tu habitación? (sí) _____

2. ¿Pones esos libros sobre el escritorio? (no) _____

3. ¿Traes los pasajes y el pasaporte al aeropuerto? (sí) _____

4. ¿Oyes ese programa de radio a veces (*sometimes*)? (no) _____

5. ¿Conoces a aquellas chicas que están tomando el sol? (sí) _____

6. ¿Pones la televisión mientras (*while*) estudias? (no) _____

2 **El tiempo** Complete these sentences with the most logical verbs from the list. Use each verb once.

cerrar	pedir	poder	querer
comenzar	pensar	preferir	volver

1. Está empezando a hacer frío. Mi mamá _____ comprar un abrigo.

2. Hace mucho sol. (Tú) _____ a buscar tus gafas de sol.

3. Hace fresco. Melissa _____ salir a pasear en bicicleta.

4. Está nevando. (Yo) _____ estar en casa hoy.

5. Está lloviendo. Luis y Pilar _____ las ventanas del auto.

6. Hace mucho calor. Ustedes _____ ir a nadar en la piscina.

7. Está nublado. Los chicos _____ temprano de la playa.

8. Llueve. Los turistas _____ un impermeable en el hotel.

3 **No son éstos** Answer these questions negatively using demonstrative pronouns.

> **modelo**
>
> ¿Les vas a prestar esos programas a ellos? (*those over there*)
> No, les voy a prestar aquéllos./No, voy a prestarles aquéllos.

1. ¿Me vas a vender esa calculadora? (*this one*)

   _____

2. ¿Van ustedes a abrirle ese auto al cliente? (*that one over there*)

   _____

3. ¿Va a llevarles estas maletas Marisol? (*those ones*)

   _____

4. ¿Les van a enseñar esos verbos a los estudiantes? (*these ones*)

4 **¿Son o están?** Form complete sentences using the words provided and **ser** or **estar**.

1. Paloma y Carlos / inteligentes y trabajadores

_____

2. Mariela / cantando una canción bonita

_____

3. (tú) / conductor de taxi en la ciudad

_____

4. (nosotros) / en un hotel en la playa

_____

5. Gilberto / preocupado porque tiene mucho trabajo

_____

6. Roberto y yo / puertorriqueños, de San Juan

_____

5 **La compra** Look at the photo and imagine everything that led up to the woman's purchase. What did she need? Why did she need it? What kind of weather is it for? Where did she decide to go buy it? Where did she go looking for it? Who helped her, and what did she ask them? Did she bargain with anyone? Was she undecided about anything? How did she pay for the purchase? Who did she pay? Answer these questions in a paragraph, using the preterite of the verbs that you know.

_____

_____

_____

_____

_____

_____

_____

_____

_____

_____

_____

_____

_____

     © 2016 by Vista Higher Learning, Inc. All rights reserved.

Bienvenida, Marissa   Lección 1

Antes de ver el video

1   **¡Mucho gusto!** In this episode, Marissa will be meeting the **familia Díaz** for the first time. Look at the image and write down what you think Marissa, Mrs. Díaz, and Mr. Díaz are saying.

_____

_____

_____

_____

_____

_____

Mientras ves el video

2   **Completar** Watch **Bienvenida, Marissa** and fill in the blanks in the following sentences.

SRA. DÍAZ ¿(1)_____ hora es?

MARISSA (2)_____ las cuatro menos diez.

DON DIEGO Buenas tardes, (3)_____. Señorita, bienvenida a la Ciudad de México.

MARISSA ¡Muchas gracias! Me (4)_____ Marissa.
¿(5)_____ se llama usted?

DON DIEGO Yo soy Diego, mucho (6)_____.

MARISSA El gusto es (7)_____, don Diego.

DON DIEGO ¿Cómo (8)_____ usted hoy, señora Carolina?

SRA. DÍAZ Muy bien, gracias, ¿y (9)_____?

DON DIEGO Bien, (10)_____.

SRA. DÍAZ Ahí hay (11)_____ maletas. Son de Marissa.

DON DIEGO Con (12)_____.

3   **¿Cierto o falso?** Indicate whether each statement is **cierto** or **falso**.

	Cierto	Falso
1. Marissa es de Wisconsin.	○	○
2. Jimena es profesora.	○	○
3. La señora Díaz es de Cuba.	○	○
4. Felipe es estudiante.	○	○
5. El señor Díaz es de la Ciudad de México.	○	○
6. Marissa no tiene (*doesn't have*) diccionario.	○	○

© 2016 by Vista Higher Learning, Inc. All rights reserved.   **Lección 1 Fotonovela** Video Activities   **1**

Después de ver el video

4 **¿Quién?** Write the name of the person who said each of the following sentences.

1. Ellos son estudiantes. _____

2. Son las cuatro y veinticinco. _____

3. Hasta luego, señor Díaz. _____

4. La chica de Wisconsin. _____

5. Bienvenida, Marissa. _____

6. Nosotros somos tu diccionario. _____

7. Hay... tres cuadernos... un mapa... un libro de español... _____

8. Marissa, te presento a Roberto, mi esposo. _____

9. De nada. _____

10. Lo siento, Marissa. _____

11. ¿Cómo se dice mediodía en inglés? _____

12. No hay de qué. _____

13. ¿Qué hay en esta cosa? _____

14. ¿Quiénes son los dos chicos de las fotos? ¿Jimena y Felipe? _____

15. Gracias, don Diego. _____

5 **Ho, ho, hola...** Imagine that you have just met the man or woman of your dreams, and that person speaks only Spanish! Don't be shy! Write what the two of you would say in your first conversation.

_____

_____

_____

_____

_____

_____

_____

6 **En la clase** Imagine that you are in Mexico studying Spanish. Write your conversation with your Spanish professor on the first day you attend the university.

_____

_____

_____

_____

_____

_____

Video Manual: Fotonovela

 © 2016 by Vista Higher Learning, Inc. All rights reserved.

¿Qué estudias?   Lección 2

Antes de ver el video

1 Impresiones Based on your impressions of Marissa, Felipe, and Jimena in **Lección 1**, write the names of the classes you think each person is taking or is most interested in. Circle the name of the person you believe is the most studious, and underline the name of the character you believe is the most talkative.

MARISSA   **FELIPE**   **JIMENA**

_____   _____   _____

_____   _____   _____

_____   _____   _____

Mientras ves el video

2 ¿Quién y a quién? Watch **¿Qué estudias?** and say who asks these questions and to whom.

Preguntas	¿Quién?	¿A quién?
1. ¿A quién buscas?	_____	_____
2. ¿Cuántas clases tomas?	_____	_____
3. ¿Qué estudias?	_____	_____
4. ¿Dónde está tu diccionario?	_____	_____
5. ¿Hablas con tu mamá?	_____	_____

3 ¿Qué cosas hay? Make a check mark beside the actions, items and places shown in **¿Qué estudias?**

____ 1. libros   ____ 5. comprar   ____ 9. pizarra

____ 2. laboratorio   ____ 6. tiza   ____ 10. dibujar

____ 3. caminar   ____ 7. hablar   ____ 11. reloj

____ 4. castillo   ____ 8. horario   ____ 12. mochila

4 Completar Fill in the blanks.

1. Marissa está en México para _____.

2. Marissa toma cuatro _____.

3. La _____ de Marissa es arqueología.

4. La especialización de Miguel es _____.

5. A Miguel le gusta _____.

6. Marissa _____ muy bien el español.

7. Juan Carlos toma química con el _____ Morales.

8. El profesor Morales enseña en un laboratorio sin _____.

9. A Felipe le gusta estar _____ el reloj y la puerta.

10. Maru _____ con su mamá.

© 2016 by Vista Higher Learning, Inc. All rights reserved.   **Lección 2 Fotonovela** Video Activities   **3**

Video Manual: *Fotonovela*

Después de ver el video

5 Corregir The underlined words in the following statements are incorrect. Fill in the blanks with the correct ones.

1. <u>Maru</u> es de los Estados Unidos. _____

2. <u>Miguel</u> toma una clase de computación. _____

3. <u>Felipe</u> necesita comprar libros. _____

4. En clase, a Marissa le gusta estar cerca <u>del reloj</u>. _____

5. <u>Felipe</u> es de Argentina. _____

6. Marissa toma español, <u>periodismo</u>, literatura y geografía. _____

7. Felipe busca a Juan Carlos y a <u>Maru</u>. _____

8. Felipe necesita practicar <u>español</u>. _____

6 Asociar Write the words or phrases in the box next to the names.

¿A la biblioteca?	cuatro clases	¿Por qué tomo química
arqueología	Ésta es la Ciudad de México.	y computación?
Buenos Aires	Hola, mamá, ¿cómo estás?	Te gusta la tarea.
ciencias ambientales	Me gusta mucho la cultura mexicana.	Y sin diccionario.

1. Marissa _____   _____

   _____

2. Felipe _____   _____

3. Juan Carlos _____   _____

   _____

4. Maru _____   _____

7 ¿Y tú? Write a paragraph saying who you are, where you are from, where you study (city and name of university), and what classes you are taking this semester.

_____

_____

_____

_____

_____

_____

_____

_____

_____

_____

  © 2016 by Vista Higher Learning, Inc. All rights reserved.

Un domingo en familia   Lección 3

Antes de ver el video

1

Examinar el título Look at the title of the episode. Based on the title and the image below, imagine what you think you will see.

_____
_____
_____
_____
_____
_____

Mientras ves el video

2

Completar Fill in the blanks for each sentence from column A with a word from column B, according to **Un domingo en familia**.

A

1. Marta _____ ocho años.
2. Las hijas de Nayeli son simpáticas y _____.
3. La _____ de Ramón y Roberto se llama Ana María.
4. Jimena dice que Felipe es _____ y feo.
5. Jimena es muy _____.
6. Ana María _____ en Mérida.

B

trabajadora
tiene
vive
gordo
bonitas
hermana

3

En Xochimilco Check off each person or thing that appears.

_____ 1. a Biology book
_____ 2. Marissa's grandparents
_____ 3. Jimena's cousins
_____ 4. a desk

_____ 5. Felipe's uncle
_____ 6. a soccer ball
_____ 7. trajineras
_____ 8. mariachis

_____ 9. people eating
_____ 10. Felipe's girlfriend
_____ 11. Jimena's dad
_____ 12. Ana María's son-in-law

4

¿Cierto o falso? Indicate whether each statement is **cierto** or **falso**.

	Cierto	Falso
1. Felipe tiene mucha hambre.	○	○
2. El ex novio de Marissa es alemán.	○	○
3. Ana María tiene tres hijos.	○	○
4. Marissa tiene una sobrina que se llama Olivia.	○	○
5. La señora Díaz dice que su cuñada es muy simpática.	○	○

Después de ver el video

Video Manual: *Fotonovela*

5 **Seleccionar** Select the letter of the word or phrase that goes in each sentence.

1. Roberto es el _____ de Felipe y Jimena.

   a. tío   b. primo   c. padre   d. sobrino

2. Los abuelos de Marissa son _____.

   a. ecuatorianos   b. españoles   c. mexicanos   d. alemanes

3. Adam es el _____ de Marissa.

   a. hermano menor   b. tío   c. primo   d. cuñado

4. Carolina tiene una _____ que se llama Ana María.

   a. tía   b. cuñada   c. hermana   d. prima

5. Las _____ de Nayeli son _____.

   a. primas; altas   b. hermanas; trabajadoras   c. hijas; simpáticas   d. sobrinas; guapas

6. La _____ de Nayeli es muy _____.

   a. sobrina; trabajadora   b. abuela; vieja   c. mamá; simpática   d. tía; alta

7. La _____ de Carolina tiene _____.

   a. tía; hambre   b. hija; sed   c. sobrina; frío   d. familia; sueño

8. Marissa decide ir a _____.

   a. la librería   b. la cafetería   c. Mérida   d. el estadio

6 **Preguntas** Answer the questions, using complete sentences.

1. ¿Quién tiene tres hermanos?

   _____

2. ¿Cuántos años tiene Valentina, la hija de Nayeli?

   _____

3. ¿Quién es hija única?

   _____

4. ¿Cómo se llama el hermano de Jimena?

   _____

5. ¿Cómo se llama el padre de Felipe?

   _____

7 **Preguntas personales** Answer the questions about your family.

1. ¿Cuántas personas hay en tu familia? ¿Cuál es más grande (*bigger*), tu familia o la familia de Jimena? _____

   _____

2. ¿Tienes hermanos/as? ¿Cómo se llaman? _____

   _____

3. ¿Tienes un(a) primo/a favorito/a? ¿Cómo es? _____

   _____

4. ¿Cómo es tu tío/a favorito/a? ¿Dónde vive? _____

   _____

© 2016 by Vista Higher Learning, Inc. All rights reserved.

Fútbol, cenotes y mole   Lección 4

Antes de ver el video

1 **El cenote** In this episode, Miguel, Maru, Marissa, and Jimena are going to a cenote to swim. What do you think they will see? What will they talk about?

_____

_____

_____

_____

_____

_____

Mientras ves el video

2 **Verbos** These sentences are taken from **Fútbol, cenotes y mole**. As you watch this segment, fill in the blanks with the missing verbs.

1. ¿No vamos a _____? ¿Qué es un cenote?

2. Ella nada y _____ al tenis y al golf.

3. Bueno, chicos, ya es hora, ¡_____!

4. Si _____, compramos el almuerzo.

3 **¿Qué ves?** Check what you see.

____ 1. una pelota de fútbol   ____ 5. un periódico

____ 2. un mensaje de correo electrónico   ____ 6. un restaurante

____ 3. una mochila   ____ 7. una plaza

____ 4. un videojuego   ____ 8. un cine

4 **Completar** Fill in the blanks in Column A with words from Column B.

A	B
1. Miguel dice que un cenote es una _____ natural.	montañas
2. Marissa dice que donde ella vive no hay _____.	pasatiempos
3. La tía Ana María tiene muchos _____ y actividades.	almorzar
4. La tía Ana María va al cine y a los _____.	museos
5. Eduardo y Pablo dicen que hay un partido de fútbol en el _____.	nadan
6. Don Guillermo dice que hay muchos _____ buenos en Mérida.	piscina
7. Felipe desea _____ mole.	restaurantes
8. Marissa y sus amigos _____ en el cenote.	parque

© 2016 by Vista Higher Learning, Inc. All rights reserved. **Lección 4 Fotonovela** Video Activities   **7**

Después de ver el video

5 **¿Qué hacen?** For numbers 1–11, fill in the missing letters in each word. For number 12, put the letters in the boxes in the right order.

1. Pablo dice que si no consigue más jugadores, su equipo va a □ __ __ d __ __.

2. Miguel dice que en México sólo hay __ __ n __ __ __ □ en la península de Yucatán.

3. Felipe dice que el restaurante del mole está en el __ __ __ □ __ o.

4. La tía Ana María sale mucho los __ __ n __ □ de semana.

5. Don Guillermo dice que hay un buen restaurante en la □ __ a __ __.

6. El mole de la tía Ana María es el __ __ v __ __ □ __ __ de Jimena.

7. Juan Carlos y Felipe van a __ __ __ □ r al fútbol con Eduardo y Pablo.

8. Eduardo juega con la p □ __ __ __ __ después del partido.

9. Eduardo y Pablo van a pagar lo que Felipe y Juan Carlos van a □ __ m __ __ __ __ __.

10. Marissa no escala □ __ __ t __ __ __ __.

11. Los chicos hablan con don Guillermo después de jugar al __ __ __ b □ __.

12. La tía Ana María tiene muchos _____.

6 **Me gusta** Fill in the chart with the activities, hobbies, or sports that you enjoy. Also say when and where you do each activity.

Mis pasatiempos favoritos	¿Cuándo?	¿Dónde?

7 **Preguntas** Answer these questions in Spanish.

1. ¿Son aficionados/as a los deportes tus amigos/as? ¿Cuáles son sus deportes favoritos?

_____

_____

2. ¿Qué hacen tú y tus amigos/as cuando tienen ratos libres?

_____

_____

3. ¿Qué vas a hacer esta noche? ¿Vas a estudiar? ¿Descansar? ¿Mirar televisión? ¿Ver una película? ¿Por qué? _____

_____

_____

    © 2016 by Vista Higher Learning, Inc. All rights reserved.

Video Manual: *Fotonovela*

¡Vamos a la playa!   Lección 5

Antes de ver el video

1 **¿Qué hacen?** The six friends have just arrived at the beach. Based on the image, what do you think Maru and Jimena are doing? What do you think they will do next?

_____

_____

_____

_____

_____

_____

_____

Mientras ves el video

2 **¿Quién?** Watch the episode and write the name of the person that goes with each expression.

Expresión	Nombre
1. En Yucatán hace mucho calor.	_____
2. ¿Están listos para su viaje a la playa?	_____
3. No podemos perder el autobús.	_____
4. Bienvenidas. ¿En qué puedo servirles?	_____
5. No está nada mal el hotel, ¿verdad? Limpio, cómodo.	_____

3 **¿Qué ves?** Check what is shown.

_____ 1. un inspector de aduanas   _____ 5. unas maletas   _____ 9. la planta baja del hotel

_____ 2. el mar   _____ 6. una pelota   _____ 10. unas llaves

_____ 3. un aeropuerto   _____ 7. una agencia de viajes _____ 11. un libro

_____ 4. un botones   _____ 8. el campo   _____ 12. personas en la playa

4 **Completar** Fill in the blanks.

1. **TÍA ANA MARÍA** Excelente, entonces… ¡A la _____!

2. **MARU** Tenemos una _____ para seis personas para esta noche.

3. **EMPLEADO** Dos _____ en el primer piso para seis huéspedes.

4. **MIGUEL** Ellos son mis amigos. Ellos sí son _____ conmigo.

5. **MARISSA** Yo estoy un poco _____. ¿Y tú? ¿Por qué no estás nadando?

© 2016 by Vista Higher Learning, Inc. All rights reserved.   **Lección 5 Fotonovela** Video Activities   **9**

Después de ver el video

5 **¿Cierto o falso?** Say whether each statement is **cierto** or **falso**. Correct the false statements.

1. Miguel está enojado con Felipe.

   _____

2. Felipe y Marissa hablan con un empleado del hotel.

   _____

3. Los ascensores del hotel están a la izquierda.

   _____

4. Maru y su novio quieren hacer windsurf, pero no tienen tablas.

   _____

5. Felipe dice que el hotel es feo y desagradable.

   _____

6. Jimena dice que estudiar en la playa es muy divertido.

   _____

6 **Resumir** Write a summary of this episode in Spanish. Try not to leave out any important information.

   _____

   _____

   _____

   _____

   _____

   _____

   _____

   _____

7 **Preguntas** Answer these questions in Spanish.

1. ¿Te gusta ir de vacaciones? ¿Por qué? _____

   _____

2. ¿Adónde te gusta ir de vacaciones? ¿Por qué? _____

   _____

3. ¿Con quién(es) vas de vacaciones? _____

   _____

 © 2016 by Vista Higher Learning, Inc. All rights reserved.

En el mercado   Lección 6

Antes de ver el video

1 **Describir** Look at the image and describe what you see, answering these questions: Where are Maru, Jimena, and Marissa? Who are they talking to? What is the purpose of their conversation?

_____

_____

_____

_____

_____

_____

Mientras ves el video

2 **Ordenar** Watch **En el mercado** and indicate the order in which you hear the following.

____ a. Acabamos de comprar tres bolsas por 480 pesos.

____ b. ¿Encontraron el restaurante?

____ c. Esta falda azul es muy elegante.

____ d. Le doy un muy buen precio.

____ e. Mira, son cuatro. Roja, amarilla, blanca, azul.

____ f. Acabo de ver una bolsa igual a ésta que cuesta 30 pesos menos.

3 **Mérida** Check each thing you see.

____ 1. una tarjeta de crédito   ____ 4. un impermeable

____ 2. una blusa   ____ 5. unos aretes

____ 3. un mercado   ____ 6. un vendedor

4 **¿Quién lo dijo?** Indicate whether Marissa, Miguel, or don Guillermo said each sentence.

_____ 1. Quiero comprarle un regalo a Maru.

_____ 2. ¿Me das aquella blusa rosada? Me parece que hace juego con esta falda.

_____ 3. ¿Puedo ver ésos, por favor?

_____ 4. Hasta más tarde. Y ¡buena suerte!

_____ 5. Me contaron que los vendedores son muy simpáticos.

Video Manual: Fotonovela

Después de ver el video

5 Completar Complete the following sentences with words from the box.

azul	hermana	novia
camisetas	mercado	regatear
en efectivo	negro	vender

1. Juan Carlos, Felipe y Miguel creen que las chicas no saben _____.

2. Los seis amigos van de compras a un _____.

3. Marissa dice que el color _____ está de moda.

4. Miguel quiere comprarle un regalo a su _____ Maru.

5. Las _____ de Juan Carlos y Felipe costaron 200 pesos.

6. Las chicas pagan 480 pesos _____ por las bolsas.

6 Corregir All these statements are false. Rewrite them so they are true.

1. Jimena dice que la ropa del mercado es muy fea.
_____

2. Marissa usa la talla 6.
_____

3. Maru compró una blusa.
_____

4. Miguel compró un abrigo para Maru.
_____

7 Preguntas Answer these questions in Spanish.

1. ¿Te gusta ir de compras? ¿Por qué? _____

2. ¿Adónde vas de compras? ¿Por qué? _____

3. ¿Con quién(es) vas de compras? ¿Por qué? _____

4. Imagina que estás en un centro comercial y que tienes mil dólares. ¿Qué vas a comprar? ¿Por qué?
_____

5. Cuando compras un auto, ¿regateas con el/la vendedor(a)? _____

© 2016 by Vista Higher Learning, Inc. All rights reserved.

Video Manual: *Fotonovela*

Panorama: Los Estados Unidos   Lección 1

Antes de ver el video

1 **Más vocabulario** Look over these useful words and expressions before you watch the video.

Vocabulario útil		
algunos *some, a few*	**espectáculos** *shows*	**millón** *million*
beisbolistas *baseball players*	**estaciones** *stations*	**mucha** *large*
comparsa *parade*	**este** *this*	**muchos** *many*
concursos *contests*	**ligas mayores** *major leagues*	**por ciento** *percent*
diseñador *designer*	**más** *more*	**su** *their*
disfraces *costumes*	**mayoría** *majority*	**tiene** *has*
escritora *writer*		

2 **Deportes** In this video, you are going to learn about some famous Dominican baseball players. In preparation, answer these questions about sports.

1. What sports are popular in the United States? _____

2. What is your favorite sport? _____

3. Do you play any sports? Which ones? _____

Mientras ves el video

3 **Cognados** Check off all the cognates you hear during the video.

___ 1. agosto   ___ 3. celebrar   ___ 5. democracia   ___ 7. festival   ___ 9. intuición

___ 2. carnaval   ___ 4. discotecas   ___ 6. famosos   ___ 8. independencia   ___ 10. populares

Después de ver el video

4 **Responder** Answer the questions in Spanish. Use complete sentences.

1. ¿Cuántos hispanos hay en Estados Unidos?

_____

2. ¿De dónde son la mayoría de los hispanos en Estados Unidos?

_____

3. ¿Quiénes son Pedro Martínez y Manny Ramírez?

_____

4. ¿Dónde hay muchas discotecas y estaciones de radio hispanas?

_____

5. ¿Qué son WADO y Latino Mix?

_____

6. ¿Es Julia Álvarez una escritora dominicana?

_____

© 2016 by Vista Higher Learning, Inc. All rights reserved.
Lección 1 Panorama cultural Video Activities   **37**

Video Manual: *Panorama cultural*

Panorama: Canadá   Lección 1

Antes de ver el video

1 Más vocabulario Look over these useful words and expressions before you watch the video.

Vocabulario útil		
bancos *banks*	hijas *daughters*	periódico *newspaper*
campo *field*	investigadora científica *research scientist*	que *that*
canal de televisión *TV station*	mantienen *maintain*	revista *magazine*
ciudad *city*	mayoría *majority*	seguridad *safety*
comunidad *community*	ofrecen *offer*	sus *her*
escuelas *schools*	otras *others*	trabajadores *workers*
estudia *studies*	pasa *spends*	vive *live*

2 Responder This video talks about the Hispanic community in Montreal. In preparation for watching the video, answer the following questions about your family's background.

1. Where were your parents born? And your grandparents? _____

2. If any of them came to the U.S. or Canada from another country, when and why did they come here?
_____

3. Are you familiar with the culture of the country of your ancestors? What do you know about their culture? Do you follow any of their traditions? Which ones? _____
_____

Mientras ves el video

3 Marcar Check off the nouns you hear while watching the video.

___ 1. apartamento   ___ 3. diario   ___ 5. horas   ___ 7. instituciones   ___ 9. lápiz

___ 2. comunidad   ___ 4. escuela   ___ 6. hoteles   ___ 8. laboratorio   ___ 10. el programa

Después de ver el video

4 ¿Cierto o falso? Indicate whether these statements are **cierto** or **falso**. Correct the false statements.

1. La mayoría de los hispanos en Montreal son de Argentina. _____

2. En Montreal no hay canales de televisión en español. _____

3. En Montreal hay hispanos importantes. _____

4. Una hispana importante en el campo de la biología es Ana María Seifert. _____

5. Ella vive con sus dos hijas en una mansión en Montreal. _____

6. Ella pasa muchas horas en el museo. _____

7. En su casa mantienen muchas tradiciones argentinas. _____

8. Ella participa en convenciones nacionales e internacionales. _____

Video Manual: *Panorama cultural*

Panorama: España   Lección 2

Antes de ver el video

1 **Más vocabulario** Look over these useful words before you watch the video.

Vocabulario útil		
antiguo *ancient*	empezar *to start*	niños *children*
blanco *white*	encierro *running of bulls*	pañuelo *neckerchief, bandana*
cabeza *head*	esta *this*	peligroso *dangerous*
calle *street*	feria *fair, festival*	periódico *newspaper*
cohete *rocket (firework)*	fiesta *party, festival*	rojo *red*
comparsa *parade*	gente *people*	ropa *clothing*
correr *to run*	gigante *giant*	toro *bull*
defenderse *to defend oneself*	mitad *half*	ver *to see*

2 **Festivales** In this video, you are going to learn about a Spanish festival. List the things you would probably do and see at a festival.

_____

_____

_____

_____

Mientras ves el video

3 **Ordenar** Number the items in the order in which they appear in the video.

_____ a. cohete   _____ c. gigante   _____ e. mitad hombre,

_____ b. cuatro mujeres en   _____ d. toros   mitad animal
    un balcón

Después de ver el video

4 **Fotos** Describe the video stills.

_____

_____

_____

_____

_____

_____

_____

Video Manual: Panorama cultural

_____
_____
_____
_____
_____

5 **Crucigrama** Complete these sentences and use the words to complete the crossword.

1. El Festival de San Fermín es la combinación de tres fiestas, una de ellas es las

   _____ comerciales.

2. Las _____ son los eventos favoritos de los niños.

3. La fiesta religiosa en honor a San Fermín, las ferias comerciales y los eventos taurinos son

   celebraciones _____.

4. Los Sanfermines es una de las _____ tradicionales españolas.

5. Las personas usan ropa blanca y _____ rojos.

6. En los encierros las personas corren delante de diecisiete _____.

7. En las comparsas hay figuras _____ hombre, mitad animal.

8. En los días del festival, hay ocho _____.

9. En las comparsas hay ocho _____.

10. Las comparsas pasan por las _____ de Pamplona.

11. Otras de las figuras tienen (*have*) enormes _____.

40 **Lección 2 Panorama cultural** Video Activities   © 2016 by Vista Higher Learning, Inc. All rights reserved.

Video Manual: Panorama cultural

Nombre _____   Fecha _____

Panorama: Ecuador   Lección 3

Antes de ver el video

1 **Más vocabulario** Look over these useful words and expressions before you watch the video.

Vocabulario útil

algunas *some*	otro *other*	todo *every*
científico *scientist*	pingüino *penguin*	tomar fotografías *to take pictures*
guía *guide*	recurso *resource*	tortuga *tortoise*

2 **Foto** Describe the video still. Write at least three sentences in Spanish.

_____

_____

_____

_____

_____

_____

3 **Predecir** Look at the video still from the previous activity and write at least two sentences in Spanish about what you think you will see in this video.

_____

_____

_____

4 **Emparejar** Find the items in the second column that correspond to the ones in the first.

_____ 1. grande   a. near

_____ 2. pequeña   b. about

_____ 3. vieja   c. here

_____ 4. también   d. big

_____ 5. aquí   e. very

_____ 6. sobre   f. old

_____ 7. muy   g. also

_____ 8. cerca de   h. small

_____ 9. para   i. for

Video Manual: *Panorama cultural*

Mientras ves el video

5 **Marcar** Check off the verbs you hear while watching the video.

_____ 1. aprender   _____ 5. escribir   _____ 9. tener

_____ 2. bailar   _____ 6. estudiar   _____ 10. tomar

_____ 3. beber   _____ 7. leer   _____ 11. vivir

_____ 4. comprar   _____ 8. recibir

Después de ver el video

6 **Responder** Answer the questions in Spanish. Use complete sentences.

1. ¿En qué océano están las islas Galápagos?

_____

_____

2. ¿Qué hacen los científicos que viven en las islas?

_____

_____

3. ¿Qué hacen los turistas que visitan las islas?

_____

_____

4. ¿Qué proyectos tiene la Fundación Charles Darwin?

_____

_____

5. ¿Cuáles son los animales más grandes que viven en las islas?

_____

_____

6. ¿Por qué son importantes estas islas?

_____

_____

7 **Preferencias** Of all the animals you saw in this video, which was your favorite? Write three sentences in Spanish describing your favorite animal.

_____

_____

_____

Panorama: México Lección 4

Antes de ver el video

1 **Más vocabulario** Look over these useful words before you watch the video.

Vocabulario útil			
día *day*	estos *these*	gente *people*	sentir *to feel*
energía *energy*	fiesta *party, celebration*	para *to*	valle *valley*

2 **Describir** In this video, you will learn about the archeological ruins of Teotihuacán where the celebration of the equinox takes place every year. Do you know what the equinox is? In English, try to write a description.

equinoccio: _____

_____

_____

3 **Categorías** Categorize the words listed in the word bank.

arqueológicos	gente	increíble	mexicanos	Teotihuacán
capital mexicana	hacen	interesante	moderno	tienen
celebrar	hombres	jóvenes	mujeres	Valle de México
ciudad	importante	Latinoamérica	niños	van
escalar				

Lugares	Personas	Verbos	Adjetivos

Mientras ves el video

4 **Marcar** Check off the pastimes you see while watching the video.

_____ 1. pasear   _____ 4. escalar (pirámides)   _____ 7. visitar monumentos

_____ 2. nadar   _____ 5. tomar el sol   _____ 8. bucear

_____ 3. patinar   _____ 6. ver películas

Video Manual: *Panorama cultural*

Después de ver el video

5 **Completar** Fill in the blanks with the appropriate word(s).

la capital mexicana	muy interesante
la celebración del equinoccio	pasean
celebrar	sentir
comienzan	sol
manos	el Valle de México

1. Teotihuacán está a cincuenta kilómetros de _____.

2. A _____ van muchos grupos de música tradicional.

3. Todos quieren _____ la energía del sol en sus _____.

4. Ir a las pirámides de Teotihuacán es una experiencia _____.

5. Las personas _____ por las ruinas.

6 **¿Cierto o falso?** Indicate whether each statement is **cierto** or **falso**. Correct the false statements.

1. Las pirámides de Teotihuacán están lejos del Valle de México.

_____

2. Muchas personas van a Teotihuacán todos los años para celebrar el equinoccio.

_____

3. Turistas de muchas nacionalidades van a la celebración.

_____

4. La gente prefiere ir a Teotihuacán los martes.

_____

5. La celebración del equinoccio termina a las cinco de la mañana.

_____

6. Las personas celebran la energía que reciben de Teotihuacán todos los años.

_____

7 **Foto** Describe the video still. Write at least three sentences in Spanish.

_____

_____

_____

_____

_____

_____

 © 2016 by Vista Higher Learning, Inc. All rights reserved.

Video Manual: *Panorama cultural*

Panorama: Puerto Rico   Lección 5

Antes de ver el video

1   **Más vocabulario** Look over these useful words before you watch the video.

Vocabulario útil		
angosto *narrow*	calle *street*	plaza *square*
antiguo *old*	escultura *sculpture*	promocionar *to promote*
artesanías *handicrafts*	exposición *exhibition*	sitio *site*
bahía *bay*	fuente *fountain*	vender *to sell*
barrio *neighborhood*		

2 **Preferencias** This video describes the attractions that San Juan, the capital of Puerto Rico, has to offer. In Spanish, list at least three things that you like to do when you visit a new city.

_____

_____

_____

_____

_____

_____

Mientras ves el video

3 **Cognados** Check off all the cognates you hear during the video.

_____ 1. aeropuerto   _____ 9. estrés

_____ 2. área   _____ 10. histórico

_____ 3. arte   _____ 11. información

_____ 4. artístico   _____ 12. nacional

_____ 5. cafés   _____ 13. permanente

_____ 6. calma   _____ 14. presidente

_____ 7. capital   _____ 15. restaurantes

_____ 8. construcciones

Video Manual: *Panorama cultural*

Después de ver el video

4 Corregir All of these statements are false. Rewrite them to correct the false information.

1. El Viejo San Juan es el barrio más moderno de la capital.

_____

2. El Morro es el centro artístico y cultural de Puerto Rico.

_____

3. Muchos artistas locales compran sus creaciones en las calles.

_____

4. En diciembre se celebra la Fiesta de la Calle San Sebastián con conciertos, exposiciones especiales de arte y un carnaval.

_____

5. En el Museo de las Américas presentan exposiciones relacionadas con la historia de Norteamérica.

_____

6. Todos los días, más de un millón de visitantes llegan al Centro de Información de Turismo del Viejo San Juan.

_____

5 Completar Complete the sentences with words from the word bank.

camina	coloniales	excelente	galerías	promociona
capital	esculturas	exposición	hermoso	

1. En la bahía de la _____ de Puerto Rico está el Castillo de San Felipe del Morro.

2. Muchas de las construcciones del Viejo San Juan son _____.

3. En la mayoría de los parques hay _____ inspiradas en la historia del país.

4. El Instituto de Cultura Puertorriqueña _____ eventos culturales en la isla.

5. Hay muchas _____ de arte y museos.

6. En el Museo de San Juan hay una _____ permanente de la historia de Puerto Rico.

6 Preferencias Of all the places in San Juan that were described, which one did you find most interesting? In Spanish, describe this place and indicate why you found it so interesting.

_____

_____

_____

_____

Video Manual: *Panorama cultural*

Panorama: Cuba   Lección 6

Antes de ver el video

1 **Más vocabulario** Look over these useful words before you watch the video.

Vocabulario útil	
conversar *to talk*	**relacionadas** *related to*
imágenes *images (in this case, of a religious nature)*	**relaciones** *relationships*
miembro *member*	**sacerdote** *priest*

2 **Responder** In this video you are going to see people visiting **santeros** to talk about their problems and their futures. In preparation for watching the video, answer the following questions about your behavior and beliefs.

1. ¿Hablas con alguien (*someone*) cuando tienes problemas? ¿Con quién?

_____

_____

_____

2. En tu opinión, ¿algunas personas pueden "ver" el futuro?

_____

_____

_____

Mientras ves el video

3 **Marcar** Check off the activities you see while watching the video.

_____ 1. hombre escribiendo

_____ 2. hombre leyendo

_____ 3. mujer corriendo

_____ 4. mujer llorando (*crying*)

_____ 5. niño jugando

_____ 6. personas bailando

_____ 7. personas caminando

_____ 8. personas cantando

_____ 9. personas conversando

© 2016 by Vista Higher Learning, Inc. All rights reserved.

Lección 6 Panorama cultural Video Activities   **47**

Video Manual: *Panorama cultural*

Después de ver el video

4   **Responder** Answer the questions in Spanish using complete sentences.

1. ¿Qué es la santería?

_____

2. ¿Quiénes son los santeros?

_____

3. ¿Qué venden en las tiendas de santería?

_____

4. ¿Para qué visitan las personas a los santeros?

_____

5. ¿Quiénes son los sacerdotes?

_____

6. ¿Qué hacen los sacerdotes cuando van a las casas de las personas?

_____

5   **¿Cierto o falso?** Indicate whether each statement is **cierto** or **falso**. Correct the false statements.

1. Cada tres horas sale un barco de La Habana con destino a Regla.

_____

2. Regla es una ciudad donde se practica la santería.

_____

3. La santería es una práctica religiosa muy común en algunos países latinoamericanos.

_____

4. Los santeros no son personas importantes en su comunidad.

_____

5. La santería es una de las tradiciones cubanas más viejas.

_____

6   **Conversación** In this video, you see a **santero** talking with a woman. In Spanish, write a short conversation. Include what the woman would ask the **santero** and how he would respond to her problems.

_____

_____

_____

_____

_____

Video Manual: *Panorama cultural*

Encuentros en la plaza

Lección 1

Antes de ver el video

1 **Vos** Most Argentinians use the pronoun **vos** instead of **tú** when talking to friends. In some cases, the verb in the **vos** form is different from the **tú** form; in others, it is the same. Look at these questions with **vos**. Can you guess what the **tú** equivalent is?

> **modelo**
> Vos: ¿Cómo te llamás?
> Tú: *¿Cómo te llamas?*

1. Y vos, ¿cómo estás?

_____

2. ¿De dónde sos?

_____

2 **¡En español!** Look at the video still. Imagine a conversation between two of these people.

¡Hola! ¿Cómo te va? _____

_____

_____

_____

_____

_____

Mientras ves el video

3 **Completar** What does Silvina say when she meets her friends? Complete these conversations.

A. (3:42–3:51)

CHICO Hola.

CHICA ¿(1)_____?

CHICA Y CHICO ¡Cuánto tiempo! (*It's been so long!*)

SILVINA Sí, hace mucho, ¿no?

CHICA ¡Qué (2)_____ verte (*to see you*)!

SILVINA ¿(3)_____ están ustedes? ¿Bien?

CHICA Y CHICO (4)_____.

B. (4:12–4:19)

SILVINA Quiero (*I want*) presentarles a mi (5)_____ Gonzalo.

CHICA Hola, ¿qué (6)_____?

GONZALO Hola. Gonzalo. ¿Tú cómo te (7)_____?

CHICA Mariana.

GONZALO (8)_____, Mariana.

Después de ver el video

4 **Ordenar** Pay attention to Silvina's actions and put them in the correct order.

_____ a. presenta una amiga a Mark

_____ b. dice (*she says*): ¿Como están ustedes? ¿Bien?

_____ c. da (*she gives*) un beso y un abrazo

_____ d. camina (*she walks*) por la Plaza de Mayo

_____ e. dice: ¡Hasta pronto!

5 **¿Quién?** Indicate who would make each of these statements.

Statements	Long-time friends at a plaza	People meeting for the first time
1. ¡Qué bueno verte!		
2. Sí, hace mucho, ¿no?		
3. Les presento a mi amigo.		
4. ¿Cómo estás?		
5. Mucho gusto.		

6 **¡Cuánto tiempo!** Write a conversation you would have with a friend whom you have not seen in a long time. Include the expressions provided.

> ¡Cuánto tiempo!   ¡Qué bueno verte!
> Hace mucho.   ¿Qué tal?

_____

_____

_____

_____

_____

7 **Encuentros en la plaza** Describe two aspects of this episode that caught your attention: people, their physical proximity, activities they do, etc. Then, explain how those are similar or different in your own culture. You may use English.

_____

_____

_____

_____

_____

_____

 © 2016 by Vista Higher Learning, Inc. All rights reserved.

Los estudios

Antes de ver el video

1 **Más vocabulario** Look over these useful words before you watch the video.

Vocabulario útil	
las ciencias biológicas y de la salud *biological and health sciences*	el cuarto año de la carrera *the fourth year of college*
las ciencias físico-matemáticas *physical and mathematical sciences*	dé clases *teaches* los estudios superiores *higher education*
¿Conoces a algún ex alumno reconocido? *¿Do you know any renowned alumni?*	la psicoterapia *psychotherapy*

2 **¡En español!** Look at the video still and answer these questions in Spanish. Carlos is in Mexico City; can you guess what place? Who is Carlos talking to? What do you think this person does?

Carlos López, México, D.F.

_____

_____

_____

_____

_____

_____

_____

Mientras ves el video

3 **Conversaciones** Complete these conversations between Carlos López and two students.

CARLOS LÓPEZ ¿(1)_____ te llamas?

ESTUDIANTE Héctor.

CARLOS LÓPEZ Héctor. ¿Y qué estudias?

ESTUDIANTE (2)_____.

CARLOS LÓPEZ ¿Y cuál es tu materia favorita?

ESTUDIANTE Este… ahorita, (3)_____ de Roma.

CARLOS LÓPEZ ¿De dónde (4)_____?

ESTUDIANTE De Corea.

CARLOS LÓPEZ De Corea. ¿Te gusta estudiar en la (5)_____?

ESTUDIANTE Sí, me gusta mucho.

CARLOS LÓPEZ ¿Qué estudias?

ESTUDIANTE Estoy estudiando (6)_____.

4 **Identificar** Indicate which area of study each of these students and alumni is likely to study or have studied.

> Ciencias Biológicas y de la Salud   Ciencias Sociales
> Ciencias Físico-Matemáticas   Humanidades

Octavio Paz
Escritor

1. _____   2. _____   3. _____

Después de ver el video

5 **Oraciones** Complete each statement with the correct option.

> autobuses   estudio   profesor
> derecho   ex alumno   residencia estudiantil
> estudiantes   México, D.F.   universidad

1. _____ es un importante centro económico y cultural.

2. La UNAM es una _____ en la Ciudad de México.

3. La UNAM es como (*like*) una ciudad con _____, policía y gobierno (*government*) propios (*own*).

4. Los _____ de la UNAM son de diferentes países.

5. Hay cuatro áreas principales de _____.

6. Manuel Álvarez Bravo es un _____ famoso de la UNAM.

6 **¡Carlos López de visita (*on a visit*)!** Imagine that Carlos López visits your school and wants to find out about the institution, campus or facilities, classes, and students. Write a brief paragraph about what you would say.

> **modelo**
>
> ¡Hola, Carlos! Me llamo Rosa Estévez y estudio en la Universidad de Toronto.
> Hay muchos estudiantes de diferentes países. Este (*This*) semestre tomo clases…

_____

_____

_____

_____

_____

 © 2016 by Vista Higher Learning, Inc. All rights reserved.

La familia

Lección 3

Video Manual: *Flash cultura*

Antes de ver el video

1 **Más vocabulario** Look over these useful words before you watch the video.

Vocabulario útil

el canelazo *typical drink from Ecuador*	**¡Qué familia tan grande tiene!** *Your family is so big!*
la casa *house*	**¡Qué grande es tu casa…!** *Your house is so big!*
Día de la Madre *Mother's Day*	**¿Quién pelea con quién?** *Who fights with whom?*
Ésta es la cocina. *This is the kitchen.*	**te muestro** *I'll show you*
Éste es un patio interior.	**Vamos.** *Let's go.*
This is an interior patio.	

2 **¡En español!** Look at the video still. Imagine what Mónica will say about families in Ecuador, and write a two- or three-sentence introduction to this episode.

Mónica, Quito

¡Hola, amigos! Bienvenidos a otra aventura de *Flash cultura*. Hoy vamos (*we are going*) a hablar de… _____

_____

_____

_____

_____

_____

_____

Mientras ves el video

3 **Identificar** Identify which family these people belong to: **los Valdivieso**, **los Bolaños**, or both.

Personas	Los Valdivieso	Los Bolaños
1. abuelos	_____	_____
2. novia	_____	_____
3. esposo	_____	_____
4. esposa	_____	_____
5. sobrinos	_____	_____
6. dos hijos y una hija	_____	_____

© 2016 by Vista Higher Learning, Inc. All rights reserved.   **Lección 3 Flash cultura** Video Activities

4 **Emparejar** Watch as Mrs. Valdivieso gives Mónica a tour of the house. Match the captions to the appropriate images.

1. _____   2. _____   3. _____

a. Y éste es el comedor…
Todos comemos aquí.

b. Vamos, te enseño el
resto de la casa.

c. Éste es un patio interior.
Aquí hacemos reuniones
familiares.

d. Finalmente, ésta es
la cocina.

e. ¿Qué están haciendo hoy
en el parque?

Después de ver el video

5 **¿Cierto o falso?** Indicate whether each statement is **cierto** (*true*) or **falso** (*false*).

1. En el parque, una familia celebra el Día de la Madre. _____
2. La familia Valdivieso representa la familia moderna y la familia Bolaños representa la familia tradicional. _____
3. Los Bolaños no viven en Quito. _____
4. Bernardo tiene animales en su casa. _____
5. Los Valdivieso toman canelazo. _____

6 **¿Qué te gusta?** Imagine that you are one of the Valdivieso children and that Mónica asks you about your likes and dislikes. Select one of the children and write a paragraph using the cues provided.

bailar   dibujar   hermanos   padres

_____
_____
_____
_____
_____

7 **Andy, un chico con novia** Andy's parents just found out that he has a girlfriend. Imagine that they are being introduced to her for the first time. Write five questions they would ask her.

_____
_____
_____
_____

 © 2016 by Vista Higher Learning, Inc. All rights reserved.

¡Fútbol en España!   Lección 4

Antes de ver el video

1   **Más vocabulario**   Look over these useful words before you watch the video.

Vocabulario útil		
la afición *fans*	nunca *never*	seguro/a *sure*
más allá *beyond*	se junta (con) *is intertwined (with)*	la válvula de escape *outlet*

2   **¡En español!**   Look at the video still. Imagine what Mari Carmen will say about soccer in Spain, and write a two- or three-sentence introduction to this episode.

Mari Carmen Ortiz, Barcelona

¡Hola, amigos! ¡Bienvenidos a *Flash cultura*! Hoy vamos a

hablar de… _____

_____

_____

_____

_____

Mientras ves el video

3   **Identificar**   You might see any of these actions in a video about soccer in Spain. Check off the items you see in this episode.

___ a. celebrar un gol (*goal*)   ___ d. hablar con un jugador famoso   ___ f. pasear en bicicleta

___ b. comer churros   ___ e. jugar al fútbol   ___ g. celebrar en las calles (*streets*)

___ c. ganar un premio (*award*)   ___ h. jugar al fútbol americano

4   **Emparejar**   Indicate which teams these people are affiliated with.

1.   2.   3.

○ Barça   ○ Barça   ○ Barça

○ Real Madrid   ○ Real Madrid   ○ Real Madrid

○ no corresponde   ○ no corresponde   ○ no corresponde

© 2016 by Vista Higher Learning, Inc. All rights reserved.   **Lección 4 Flash cultura** Video Activities   **85**

Después de ver el video

5 **Completar** Complete each statement with the correct option.

| aficionados al fútbol | churros | estadio | gol | Red Sox |

1. En España hay muchos _____.

2. Camp Nou es un _____ en Barcelona.

3. La rivalidad entre el Barça y el Real Madrid es comparable con la rivalidad entre los Yankees y los _____ en béisbol.

4. Mari Carmen compra _____.

6 **Aficionados** Who are these fans? Imagine what they would say if they introduced themselves. Write information like their name, age, origin, team affiliation, and any other details that come to mind.

> **modelo**
>
> **Aficionado:** ¡Hola! Soy José Artigas y soy de Madrid. Mi equipo favorito es el Real Madrid. Miro todos los partidos en el estadio. ¡VIVA EL REAL MADRID! ¡Nunca pierde!

_____
_____
_____
_____
_____
_____
_____
_____
_____

7 **Un futbolista** Imagine that you are Mari Carmen and you decide to interview a famous soccer player in Spain. Write five questions you would ask him.

> **modelo**
>
> ¿Dónde prefieres vivir?

_____
_____
_____
_____

  © 2016 by Vista Higher Learning, Inc. All rights reserved.

¡Vacaciones en Perú!

Antes de ver el video

1 **Más vocabulario** Look over these useful words before you watch the video.

Vocabulario útil		
aislado/a *isolated*	disfrutar *to enjoy*	se salvó *was saved*
andino/a *Andean*	el esfuerzo *effort*	la selva *jungle*
ayudó *helped*	hemos contratado *we have hired*	subir *to climb, to go up*
el cultivo *farming*	la obra *work (of art)*	la vuelta al mundo *around the world*

2 **Completar** Complete these sentences. Make the necessary changes.

1. Machu Picchu es una _____ muy importante de la civilización inca.

   Esta (*This*) ciudad inca está rodeada (*surrounded*) de una gran _____.

2. Los incas fueron (*were*) grandes artistas y expertos en técnicas de _____

   como el sistema de terrazas (*terraces*).

3. Hoy muchos turistas van a _____ de las ruinas incas y del maravilloso

   paisaje andino.

4. Cada año miles de personas deciden _____ hasta Machu Picchu por el Camino Inca.

3 **¡En español!** Look at the video still. Imagine what Omar will say about Machu Picchu, and write a two- or three-sentence introduction to this episode.

Omar Fuentes, Perú

¡Bienvenidos a otra aventura de *Flash cultura*! Hoy estamos en…

_____

_____

_____

_____

Mientras ves el video

4 **Descripción** What does Noemí say about the lost city of Machu Picchu? Complete this quote.

"Omar, te cuento (*let me tell you*) que Machu Picchu se salvó de la invasión (1)_____

gracias a que se encuentra (*it's located*) (2)_____ sobre esta (3)_____,

como tú puedes ver. Y también la (4)_____ ayudó mucho… lo cubrió (*covered*)

rápidamente, y eso también contribuye."

© 2016 by Vista Higher Learning, Inc. All rights reserved. **Lección 5 Flash cultura** Video Activities **87**

5 **Emparejar** Watch the tourists describe their impressions of Machu Picchu. Match the captions to the appropriate people.

1. _____ 2. _____

3. _____ 4. _____

    a. enigma y misterio   b. magnífico y misterioso   c. algo esplendoroso, algo único…

    d. ¡Fantástico!   e. Nos encanta muchísimo.

Después de ver el video

6 **¿Cierto o falso?** Indicate whether each statement is **cierto** or **falso**.

    1. Las ruinas de Machu Picchu están al lado del mar.   _____

    2. Hay menos de (*less than*) cien turistas por día en el santuario (*sanctuary*) inca.   _____

    3. Cuando visitas Machu Picchu, puedes contratar a un guía experto.   _____

    4. Todos los turistas llegan a Machu Picchu en autobús.   _____

    5. Omar pregunta a los turistas por qué visitan Machu Picchu.   _____

7 **¡La vuelta al mundo!** Imagine that you are a travel agent and that the French globetrotting family you saw in the video is planning their next destination. Write a conversation between you and the mother. Suggest an exciting destination, describe the activities the family can do together, and then work out how to get there, where to stay, and for how long.

_____

_____

_____

_____

_____

_____

 © 2016 by Vista Higher Learning, Inc. All rights reserved.

Comprar en los mercados

Antes de ver el video

1 **Más vocabulario** Look over these useful words before you watch the video.

Vocabulario útil		
las artesanías *handicrafts*	la heladería *ice-cream shop*	la soda (C.R.) *food stall*
el camarón *shrimp*	el helado *ice cream*	la sopa de mondongo *tripe soup*
la carne *meat*	el pescado *fish*	suave *soft*
la flor *flower*	¡Pura vida! *Cool!, Alright!*	el/la tico/a *person from Costa Rica*
la fruta *fruit*	el regateo *haggling, bargaining*	vale *it costs*

2 **¡En español!** Look at the video still. Imagine what Randy will say about markets in Costa Rica, and write a two- or three-sentence introduction to this episode.

Randy Cruz, Costa Rica

¡Hola a todos! Hoy estamos en… _____

_____

_____

_____

_____

Mientras ves el video

3 **¿Qué compran?** Identify which item(s) these people buy at the market.

1. _____ 2. _____ 3. _____

a. frutas   b. artesanías   c. carne y pescado

d. camarones y flores   e. zapatos

4 **Completar** Watch Randy bargain, and complete this conversation.

RANDY ¿(1)_____ vale?

VENDEDOR Trescientos (*300*) (2)_____.

RANDY Trescientos colones el kilo. Me puede hacer un (3)_____, ¿sí?

VENDEDOR Perfecto.

VENDEDOR OK... (4)_____ cuatro ochenta... cuatro y medio.

RANDY Cuatrocientos (*400*).

VENDEDOR Cuatro (5)_____.

RANDY Cuatrocientos cuarenta.

VENDEDOR Sí, señor.

Después de ver el video

5 **Ordenar** Put Randy's actions in the correct order.

_____ a. Busca la heladería en el Mercado Central.

_____ b. Regatea el precio de unas papayas.

_____ c. Va al mercado al aire libre.

_____ d. Entrevista a personas en el Mercado Central.

_____ e. Toma sopa de mondongo, un plato (*dish*) típico de Costa Rica.

6 **¡Aquí no hay descuentos!** Imagine that Randy wants to buy an item of clothing that he really likes, but he doesn't have enough money to pay the full price. Write a conversation between Randy and a salesperson in which Randy negotiates the price. Be creative!

_____

_____

_____

_____

_____

7 **Preguntas** Answer these questions.

1. ¿En qué lugares o tipos de tiendas haces las compras generalmente? ¿Pequeñas tiendas, grandes almacenes o centros comerciales? _____

_____

2. ¿Con quién(es) sales generalmente a comprar ropa: solo/a (*alone*), con amigos o con alguien (*someone*) de tu familia? ¿Por qué? _____

_____

3. ¿Cómo prefieres pagar tus compras: en efectivo o con tarjeta de crédito? ¿Por qué? _____

_____

4. ¿Esperas las rebajas para comprar cosas que quieres o no te importa (*you don't mind*) pagar el precio normal? _____

 © 2016 by Vista Higher Learning, Inc. All rights reserved.

contextos   Lección 1

1 **Identificar** You will hear six short exchanges. For each one, decide whether it is a greeting, an introduction, or a leave-taking. Mark the appropriate column with an **X**.

> **modelo**
>
> *You hear:* RAQUEL David, te presento a Paulina.
>   DAVID Encantado.
> *You mark:* an **X** under *Introduction*.

	Greeting	*Introduction*	*Leave-taking*
Modelo	_____	**X**	_____
1.	_____	_____	_____
2.	_____	_____	_____
3.	_____	_____	_____
4.	_____	_____	_____
5.	_____	_____	_____
6.	_____	_____	_____

2 **Asociar** You will hear three conversations. Look at the drawing and write the number of the conversation under the appropriate group of people.

c. _____

b. _____

a. _____

3 **Preguntas** Listen to each question or statement and respond with an answer from the list in your lab manual. Repeat the correct response after the speaker.

a. Bien, gracias.   c. Lo siento.   e. Nada.
b. Chau.   d. Mucho gusto.   f. Soy de los Estados Unidos.

© 2016 by Vista Higher Learning, Inc. All rights reserved.   **Lección 1** Lab Activities   **1**

pronunciación

The Spanish alphabet

The Spanish and English alphabets are almost identical, with a few exceptions. For example, the Spanish letter **ñ (eñe)** doesn't occur in the English alphabet. Furthermore, the letters **k (ka)** and **w (doble ve)** are used only in words of foreign origin. Examine the chart below to find other differences.

Letra	Nombre(s)	Ejemplo(s)	Letra	Nombre(s)	Ejemplo(s)
a	a	**a**diós	n	ene	**n**acionalidad
b	be	**b**ien, pro**b**lema	ñ	eñe	ma**ñ**ana
c	ce	**c**osa, **c**ero	o	o	**o**nce
ch*	che	**ch**ico	p	pe	**p**rofesor
d	de	**d**iario, na**d**a	q	cu	**q**ué
e	e	**e**studiante	r	ere	**r**egular, seño**r**a
f	efe	**f**oto	s	ese	**s**eñor
g	ge	**g**racias, **G**erardo, re**g**ular	t	te	**t**ú
h	hache	**h**ola	u	u	**u**sted
i	i	**i**gualmente	v	ve	**v**ista, nue**v**o
j	jota	**J**avier	w	doble ve	*walkman*
k	ka, ca	**k**ilómetro	x	equis	e**x**istir, Mé**x**ico
l	ele	**l**ápiz	y	i griega, ye	**y**o
ll*	elle	**ll**ave	z	zeta, ceta	**z**ona
m	eme	**m**apa			

* Ch and ll are no longer considered separate letters.

1 **El alfabeto** Repeat the Spanish alphabet and example words after the speaker.

2 **Práctica** When you hear the number, say the corresponding word aloud and then spell it. Then listen to the speaker and repeat the correct response.

1. nada	6. por favor	11. Javier
2. maleta	7. San Fernando	12. Ecuador
3. quince	8. Estados Unidos	13. Maite
4. muy	9. Puerto Rico	14. gracias
5. hombre	10. España	15. Nueva York

3 **Dictado** You will hear six people introduce themselves. Listen carefully and write the people's names as they spell them.

1. _____

2. _____

3. _____

4. _____

5. _____

6. _____

  © 2016 by Vista Higher Learning, Inc. All rights reserved.

estructura

1.1 Nouns and articles

1 **Identificar** You will hear a series of words. Decide whether the word is masculine or feminine, and mark an **X** in the appropriate column.

> **modelo**
>
> *You hear:* lección
> *You mark:* an **X** under *feminine*.

	Masculine	Feminine
Modelo	_____	X
1.	_____	_____
2.	_____	_____
3.	_____	_____
4.	_____	_____
5.	_____	_____
6.	_____	_____
7.	_____	_____
8.	_____	_____

2 **Transformar** Change each word from the masculine to the feminine. Repeat the correct answer after the speaker. (*6 items*)

> **modelo**
>
> el chico
> la chica

3 **Cambiar** Change each word from the singular to the plural. Repeat the correct answer after the speaker. (*8 items*)

> **modelo**
>
> una palabra
> unas palabras

4 **Completar** Listen as Silvia reads her shopping list. Write the missing words in your lab manual.

_____ diccionario

un _____

_____ cuadernos

_____ mapa de _____

_____ lápices

© 2016 by Vista Higher Learning, Inc. All rights reserved.   **Lección 1** Lab Activities   **3**

1.2 Numbers 0–30

1 **¡Bingo!** You are going to play two games (**juegos**) of bingo. As you hear each number, mark it with an **X** on your bingo card.

Juego 1		
1	3	5
29	25	6
14	18	17
9	12	21

Juego 2		
0	30	27
10	3	2
16	19	4
28	22	20

2 **Números** Use the cue in your lab manual to tell how many there are of each item. Repeat the correct response after the speaker.

> **modelo**
> *You see:* 18 chicos
> *You say:* dieciocho chicos

1. 15 lápices
2. 4 computadoras
3. 8 cuadernos
4. 22 días
5. 9 lecciones
6. 30 fotos
7. 1 palabra
8. 26 diccionarios
9. 12 países
10. 3 problemas
11. 17 escuelas
12. 25 turistas

3 **Completar** You will hear a series of math problems. Write the missing numbers and solve the problems.

1. _____ + _____11_____ = _____

2. _____ – _____5_____ = _____

3. _____8_____ + _____ = _____

4. _____ – _____12_____ = _____

5. _____3_____ + _____ = _____

6. _____ + _____0_____ = _____

4 **Preguntas** Look at the drawing and answer each question you hear. Repeat the correct response after the speaker. (*6 items*)

 © 2016 by Vista Higher Learning, Inc. All rights reserved.

1.3 Present tense of **ser**

1 **Identificar** Listen to each sentence and mark an **X** in the column for the subject of the verb.

> *modelo*
>
> *You hear*: Son pasajeros.
> *You mark*: an **X** under **ellos**.

	yo	tú	él	nosotros	ellos
Modelo	___	___	___	___	X ___
1.	___	___	___	___	___
2.	___	___	___	___	___
3.	___	___	___	___	___
4.	___	___	___	___	___
5.	___	___	___	___	___
6.	___	___	___	___	___

2 **Cambiar** Form a new sentence using the cue you hear as the subject. Repeat the correct answer after the speaker. (*8 items*)

> *modelo*
>
> Isabel es de los Estados Unidos. (yo)
> *Yo soy de los Estados Unidos.*

3 **Escoger** Listen to each question and choose the most logical response.

1. a. Soy Patricia.   b. Es la señora Gómez.
2. a. Es de California.   b. Él es conductor.
3. a. Es de Canadá.   b. Es un diccionario.
4. a. Es de Patricia.   b. Soy estudiante.
5. a. Él es conductor.   b. Es de España.
6. a. Es un cuaderno.   b. Soy de los Estados Unidos.

4 **Preguntas** Answer each question you hear using the cue in your lab manual. Repeat the correct response after the speaker.

> *modelo*
>
> *You hear*: ¿De dónde es Pablo?
> *You see*: Estados Unidos
> *You say*: *Él es de los Estados Unidos.*

1. España   2. California   3. México   4. Ecuador   5. Puerto Rico   6. Colorado

5 **¿Quiénes son?** Listen to this conversation and write the answers to the questions in your lab manual.

1. ¿Cómo se llama el hombre? _____   4. ¿De dónde es ella? _____
2. ¿Cómo se llama la mujer? _____   5. ¿Quién es estudiante? _____
3. ¿De dónde es él? _____   6. ¿Quién es profesor? _____

© 2016 by Vista Higher Learning, Inc. All rights reserved.

1.4 Telling time

1   **La hora**   Look at the clock and listen to the statement. Indicate whether the statement is **cierto** or **falso**.

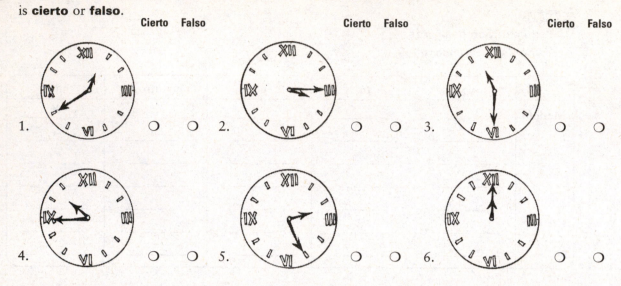

	Cierto	Falso			Cierto	Falso			Cierto	Falso
1.	○	○	2.		○	○	3.		○	○
4.	○	○	5.		○	○	6.		○	○

2   **Preguntas**   Some people want to know what time it is. Answer their questions, using the cues in your lab manual. Repeat the correct response after the speaker.

> **modelo**
>
> *You hear:* ¿Qué hora es, por favor?
> *You see:* 3:10 p.m.
> *You say:* Son las tres y diez de la tarde.

1. 1:30 p.m.   3. 2:05 p.m.   5. 4:54 p.m.

2. 9:06 a.m.   4. 7:15 a.m.   6. 10:23 p.m.

3   **¿A qué hora?**   You are trying to plan your class schedule. Ask your counselor what time these classes meet and write the answer.

> **modelo**
>
> *You see:* la clase de economía
> *You say:* ¿A qué hora es la clase de economía?
> *You hear:* Es a las once y veinte de la mañana.
> *You write:* 11:20 a.m.

1. la clase de biología: _____   4. la clase de literatura: _____

2. la clase de arte: _____   5. la clase de historia: _____

3. la clase de matemáticas: _____   6. la clase de sociología: _____

vocabulario

You will now hear the vocabulary found in your textbook on the last page of this lesson. Listen and repeat each Spanish word or phrase after the speaker.

         © 2016 by Vista Higher Learning, Inc. All rights reserved.

contextos

Lección 2

1   Identificar Look at each drawing and listen to the statement. Indicate whether the statement is **cierto** or **falso**.

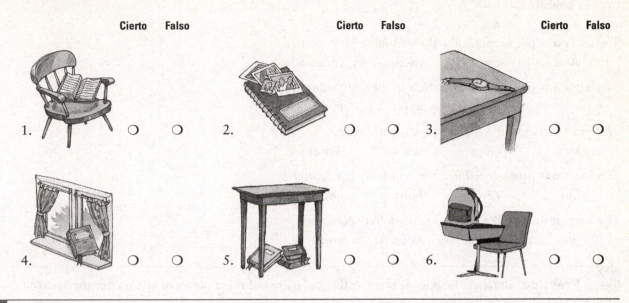

	Cierto	Falso		Cierto	Falso		Cierto	Falso
1.	○	○	2.	○	○	3.	○	○
4.	○	○	5.	○	○	6.	○	○

2   ¿Qué día es? Your friend Diego is never sure what day of the week it is. Respond to his questions saying that it is the day before the one he mentions. Then repeat the correct answer after the speaker. (6 items)

> **modelo**
> Hoy es domingo, ¿no?
> No, hoy es sábado.

3   Preguntas You will hear a series of questions. Look at Susana's schedule for today and answer each question. Then repeat the correct response after the speaker.

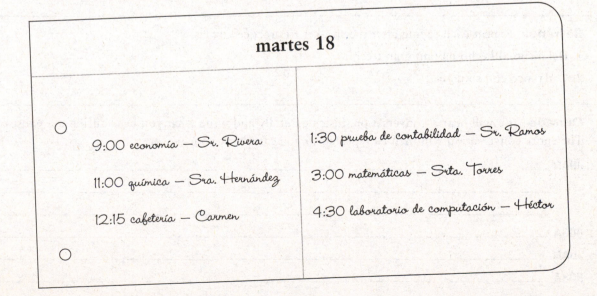

martes 18

○

9:00 economía — Sr. Rivera

11:00 química — Sra. Hernández

12:15 cafetería — Carmen

1:30 prueba de contabilidad — Sr. Ramos

3:00 matemáticas — Srta. Torres

4:30 laboratorio de computación — Héctor

○

© 2016 by Vista Higher Learning, Inc. All rights reserved.   **Lección 2** Lab Activities   **7**

pronunciación

Spanish vowels

Spanish vowels are never silent; they are always pronounced in a short, crisp way without the glide sounds used in English.

    a   **e**   **i**   **o**   **u**

The letter **a** is pronounced like the *a* in *father*, but shorter.

    Álex   cl**a**se   n**a**d**a**   enc**a**nt**a**d**a**

The letter **e** is pronounced like the *e* in *they*, but shorter.

    el   **e**n**e**   m**e**sa   **e**l**e**fant**e**

The letter **i** sounds like the *ee* in *beet*, but shorter.

    Inés   ch**i**ca   t**i**za   señor**i**ta

The letter **o** is pronounced like the *o* in *tone*, but shorter.

    h**o**la   c**o**n   libr**o**   d**o**n Francisc**o**

The letter **u** sounds like the *oo* in *room*, but shorter.

    uno   reg**u**lar   sal**u**dos   g**u**sto

1   **Práctica** Practice the vowels by repeating the names of these places in Spain after the speaker.

1. Madrid   5. Barcelona
2. Alicante   6. Granada
3. Tenerife   7. Burgos
4. Toledo   8. La Coruña

2   **Oraciones** Repeat each sentence after the speaker, focusing on the vowels.

1. Hola. Me llamo Ramiro Morgado.
2. Estudio arte en la Universidad de Salamanca.
3. Tomo también literatura y contabilidad.
4. Ay, tengo clase en cinco minutos. ¡Nos vemos!

3   **Refranes** Repeat each saying after the speaker to practice vowels.

1. Del dicho al hecho hay un gran trecho.
2. Cada loco con su tema.

4   **Dictado** You will hear a conversation. Listen carefully and write what you hear during the pauses. The entire conversation will then be repeated so you can check your work.

JUAN _____

_____

_____

ROSA _____

JUAN _____

ROSA _____

       © 2016 by Vista Higher Learning, Inc. All rights reserved.

estructura

2.1 Present tense of **-ar** verbs

1 **Identificar** Listen to each sentence and mark an **X** in the column for the subject of the verb.

> *modelo*
>
> *You hear:* Trabajo en la cafetería.
> *You mark:* an **X** under **yo**.

	yo	tú	él/ella	nosotros/as	ellos/ellas
Modelo	X	___	___	___	___
1.	___	___	___	___	___
2.	___	___	___	___	___
3.	___	___	___	___	___
4.	___	___	___	___	___
5.	___	___	___	___	___
6.	___	___	___	___	___
7.	___	___	___	___	___
8.	___	___	___	___	___

2 **Cambiar** Form a new sentence using the cue you hear as the subject. Repeat the correct answer after the speaker. (6 *items*)

> *modelo*
>
> María practica los verbos ahora. (José y María)
> *José y María practican los verbos ahora.*

3 **Preguntas** Answer each question you hear in the negative. Repeat the correct response after the speaker. (8 *items*)

> *modelo*
>
> ¿Estudias geografía?
> *No, yo no estudio geografía.*

4 **Completar** Listen to the following description and write the missing words in your lab manual.

Teresa y yo (1) _____ en la Universidad Autónoma de Madrid. Teresa

(2) _____ lenguas extranjeras. Ella (3) _____ trabajar

en las Naciones Unidas (*United Nations*). Yo (4) _____ clases de periodismo.

También me gusta (5) _____ y (6) _____. Los sábados

(7) _____ con una tuna. Una tuna es una orquesta (*orchestra*) estudiantil.

Los jóvenes de la tuna (8) _____ por las calles (*streets*) y

(9) _____ canciones (*songs*) tradicionales de España.

2.2 Forming questions in Spanish

1 **Escoger** Listen to each question and choose the most logical response.

1. a. Porque mañana es la prueba. b. Porque no hay clase mañana.
2. a. Viaja en autobús. b. Viaja a Toledo.
3. a. Llegamos el 3 de abril. b. Llegamos al estadio.
4. a. Isabel y Diego dibujan. b. Dibujan en la clase de arte.
5. a. No, enseña física. b. No, enseña en la Universidad Politécnica.
6. a. Escuchan un video. b. Escuchan música clásica.
7. a. Sí, me gusta mucho. b. Miro la televisión en la residencia.
8. a. Hay diccionarios en la biblioteca. b. Hay tres.

2 **Cambiar** Change each sentence into a question using the cue in your lab manual. Repeat the correct response after the speaker.

> **modelo**
>
> *You hear:* Los turistas toman el autobús.
> *You see:* ¿Quiénes?
> *You say:* ¿Quiénes toman el autobús?

1. ¿Dónde?   3. ¿Qué?, (tú)   5. ¿Cuándo?   7. ¿Quiénes?
2. ¿Cuántos?   4. ¿Quién?   6. ¿Dónde?   8. ¿Qué?, (tú)

3 **¿Lógico o ilógico?** You will hear some questions and the responses. Decide if they are **lógico** (*logical*) or **ilógico** (*illogical*).

1. Lógico   Ilógico   3. Lógico   Ilógico   5. Lógico   Ilógico
2. Lógico   Ilógico   4. Lógico   Ilógico   6. Lógico   Ilógico

4 **Un anuncio** Listen to this radio advertisement and answer the questions in your lab manual.

1. ¿Dónde está (*is*) la Escuela Cervantes? _____
_____

2. ¿Qué cursos ofrecen (*do they offer*) en la Escuela Cervantes? _____
_____

3. ¿Cuándo practican los estudiantes el español? _____
_____

4. ¿Adónde viajan los estudiantes de la Escuela Cervantes? _____
_____

© 2016 by Vista Higher Learning, Inc. All rights reserved.

2.3 Present tense of **estar**

1 **Describir** Look at the drawing and listen to each statement. Indicate whether the statement is **cierto** or **falso**.

	Cierto	Falso		Cierto	Falso		Cierto	Falso
1.	○	○	3.	○	○	5.	○	○
2.	○	○	4.	○	○	6.	○	○

2 **Cambiar** Form a new sentence using the cue you hear. Repeat the correct answer after the speaker. (*8 items*)

> **modelo**
> Irma está en la biblioteca. (Irma y Hugo)
> *Irma y Hugo están en la biblioteca.*

3 **Escoger** You will hear some sentences with a beep in place of the verb. Decide which form of **ser** or **estar** should complete each sentence and circle it.

> **modelo**
> *You hear:* Javier (*beep*) estudiante.
> *You circle:* **es** because the sentence is **Javier es estudiante**.

1. es   está   5. es   está
2. es   está   6. eres   estás
3. es   está   7. son   están
4. Somos   Estamos   8. Son   Están

2.4 Numbers 31 and higher

1 **Números de teléfono** You want to invite some classmates to a party, but you don't have their telephone numbers. Ask the person who sits beside you what their telephone numbers are, and write the answer.

> **modelo**
>
> *You see:* Elián
> *You say:* ¿Cuál es el número de teléfono de Elián?
> *You hear:* Es el ocho, cuarenta y tres, cero, ocho, treinta y cinco.
> *You write:* 843-0835

1. Arturo: _____   5. Simón: _____

2. Alicia: _____   6. Eva: _____

3. Roberto: _____   7. José Antonio: _____

4. Graciela: _____   8. Mariana: _____

2 **Dictado** Listen carefully and write each number as numerals rather than words.

1. _____   4. _____   7. _____

2. _____   5. _____   8. _____

3. _____   6. _____   9. _____

3 **Mensaje telefónico** Listen to this telephone conversation and complete the phone message in your lab manual with the correct information.

Mensaje telefónico

_____

Para (*For*) _____

De parte de (*From*) _____

Teléfono _____

Mensaje _____

_____

_____

_____

---

vocabulario

You will now hear the vocabulary found in your textbook on the last page of this lesson. Listen and repeat each Spanish word or phrase after the speaker.

© 2016 by Vista Higher Learning, Inc. All rights reserved.

contextos

Lección 3

1 **Escoger** You will hear some questions. Look at the family tree and choose the correct answer to each question.

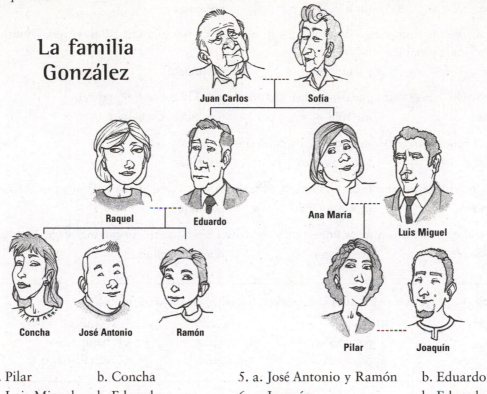

La familia
González

Juan Carlos   Sofía

Raquel   Eduardo   Ana María

Luis Miguel

Concha   José Antonio   Ramón

Pilar   Joaquín

1. a. Pilar   b. Concha   5. a. José Antonio y Ramón   b. Eduardo y Ana María

2. a. Luis Miguel   b. Eduardo   6. a. Joaquín   b. Eduardo

3. a. Sofía   b. Ana María   7. a. Ana María   b. Sofía

4. a. Raquel   b. Sofía   8. a. Luis Miguel   b. Juan Carlos

2 **La familia González** Héctor wants to verify the relationship between various members of the González family. Look at the drawing and answer his questions with the correct information. Repeat the correct response after the speaker. (*6 items*)

> **modelo**
>
> Juan Carlos es el abuelo de Eduardo, ¿verdad?
> No, Juan Carlos es el padre de Eduardo.

3 **Profesiones** Listen to each statement and write the number of the statement below the drawing it describes.

a. _____   b. _____   c. _____   d. _____

© 2016 by Vista Higher Learning, Inc. All rights reserved.

pronunciación

Diphthongs and linking

In Spanish, **a**, **e**, and **o** are considered strong vowels. The weak vowels are **i** and **u**.

    herm**a**no   n**i**ña   cuñ**a**do

A diphthong is a combination of two weak vowels or of a strong vowel and a weak vowel. Diphthongs are pronounced as a single syllable.

    r**ui**do   par**ie**ntes   per**io**dista

Two identical vowel sounds that appear together are pronounced like one long vowel.

    l**a a**buela   m**i hi**jo   una clas**e e**xcelente

Two identical consonants together sound like a single consonant.

    co**n N**atalia   su**s s**obrinos   la**s s**illas

A consonant at the end of a word is always linked with the vowel sound at the beginning of the next word.

    E**s i**ngeniera.   mi**s a**buelos   su**s h**ijos

A vowel at the end of a word is always linked with the vowel sound at the beginning of the next word.

    m**i h**ermano   s**u e**sposa   nuestr**o a**migo

1 **Práctica** Repeat each word after the speaker, focusing on the diphthongs.

1. historia
2. nieto
3. parientes
4. novia
5. residencia
6. prueba
7. puerta
8. ciencias
9. lenguas
10. estudiar
11. izquierda
12. ecuatoriano

2 **Oraciones** When you hear the number, read the corresponding sentence aloud. Then listen to the speaker and repeat the sentence.

1. Hola. Me llamo Anita Amaral. Soy del Ecuador.
2. Somos seis en mi familia.
3. Tengo dos hermanos y una hermana.
4. Mi papá es del Ecuador y mi mamá es de España.

3 **Refranes** Repeat each saying after the speaker to practice diphthongs and linking sounds.

1. Cuando una puerta se cierra, otra se abre.
2. Hablando del rey de Roma, por la puerta se asoma.

4 **Dictado** You will hear eight sentences. Each will be said twice. Listen carefully and write what you hear.

1. _____
2. _____
3. _____
4. _____
5. _____
6. _____
7. _____
8. _____

© 2016 by Vista Higher Learning, Inc. All rights reserved.

estructura

3.1 Descriptive adjectives

1 **Transformar** Change each sentence from the masculine to the feminine. Repeat the correct answer after the speaker. (6 *items*)

> *modelo*
> El chico es mexicano.
> La *chica es mexicana.*

2 **Cambiar** Change each sentence from the singular to the plural. Repeat the correct answer after the speaker. (6 *items*)

> *modelo*
> El profesor es ecuatoriano.
> Los *profesores son ecuatorianos.*

3 **Mis compañeros de clase** Describe your classmates, using the cues in your lab manual. Repeat the correct response after the speaker.

> *modelo*
> *You hear:* María
> *You see:* alto
> *You say:* María es alta.

1. simpático
2. rubio
3. inteligente
4. pelirrojo y muy bonito
5. alto y moreno
6. delgado y trabajador
7. bajo y gordo
8. tonto

4 **Completar** Listen to the following description and write the missing words in your lab manual.

Mañana mis parientes llegan de Guayaquil. Son cinco personas: mi abuela Isabel, tío Carlos y tía Josefina, y mis primos Susana y Tomás. Mi prima es (1)_____ y (2)_____. Baila muy bien. Tomás es un niño (3)_____, pero es (4)_____. Tío Carlos es (5)_____ y (6)_____. Tía Josefina es (7)_____ y (8)_____. Mi abuela es (9)_____ y muy (10)_____.

5 **La familia Rivas** Look at the photo of the Rivas family and listen to each statement. Indicate whether the statement is **cierto** or **falso**.

	Cierto	Falso
1.	○	○
2.	○	○
3.	○	○
4.	○	○
5.	○	○
6.	○	○
7.	○	○

© 2016 by Vista Higher Learning, Inc. All rights reserved.

3.2 Possessive adjectives

1 **Identificar** Listen to each statement and mark an **X** in the column for the possessive adjective you hear.

modelo

> You hear: Es mi diccionario de español.
> You mark: an **X** under **my**.

	my	your (familiar)	your (formal)	his/her	our	their
Modelo	X	_____	_____	_____	_____	_____
1.	_____	_____	_____	_____	_____	_____
2.	_____	_____	_____	_____	_____	_____
3.	_____	_____	_____	_____	_____	_____
4.	_____	_____	_____	_____	_____	_____
5.	_____	_____	_____	_____	_____	_____
6.	_____	_____	_____	_____	_____	_____
7.	_____	_____	_____	_____	_____	_____
8.	_____	_____	_____	_____	_____	_____

2 **Escoger** Listen to each question and choose the most logical response.

1. a. No, su hijastro no está aquí.
   b. Sí, tu hijastro está aquí.
2. a. No, nuestros abuelos son argentinos.
   b. Sí, sus abuelos son norteamericanos.
3. a. Sí, tu hijo trabaja ahora.
   b. Sí, mi hijo trabaja en la librería Goya.
4. a. Sus padres regresan hoy a las nueve.
   b. Mis padres regresan hoy a las nueve.
5. a. Nuestra hermana se llama Margarita.
   b. Su hermana se llama Margarita.
6. a. Tus plumas están en el escritorio.
   b. Sus plumas están en el escritorio.
7. a. No, mi sobrino es ingeniero.
   b. Sí, nuestro sobrino es programador.
8. a. Su horario es muy bueno.
   b. Nuestro horario es muy bueno.

3 **Preguntas** Answer each question you hear in the affirmative using the appropriate possessive adjective. Repeat the correct response after the speaker. (*7 items*)

modelo

> ¿Es tu lápiz?
> Sí, *es mi lápiz.*

   © 2016 by Vista Higher Learning, Inc. All rights reserved.

3.3 Present tense of -er and -ir verbs

1 Identificar Listen to each statement and mark an **X** in the column for the subject of the verb.

> **modelo**
> *You hear*: Corro con Dora mañana.
> *You mark*: an **X** under **yo**.

	yo	tú	él/ella	nosotros/as	ellos/ellas
Modelo	X	_____	_____	_____	_____
1.	_____	_____	_____	_____	_____
2.	_____	_____	_____	_____	_____
3.	_____	_____	_____	_____	_____
4.	_____	_____	_____	_____	_____
5.	_____	_____	_____	_____	_____
6.	_____	_____	_____	_____	_____

2 Cambiar Listen to the following statements. Using the cues you hear, say that these people do the same activities. Repeat the correct answer after the speaker. (*8 items*)

> **modelo**
> Julia aprende francés. (mi amigo)
> *Mi amigo también aprende francés.*

3 Preguntas Answer each question you hear in the negative. Repeat the correct response after the speaker. (*8 items*)

> **modelo**
> ¿Viven ellos en una residencia estudiantil?
> *No, ellos no viven en una residencia estudiantil.*

4 Describir Listen to each statement and write the number of the statement below the drawing it describes.

a. _____   b. _____   c. _____   d. _____

© 2016 by Vista Higher Learning, Inc. All rights reserved.   **Lección 3** Lab Activities

3.4 Present tense of **tener** and **venir**

1 **Cambiar** Form a new sentence using the cue you hear as the subject. Repeat the correct answer after the speaker. (6 *items*)

> *modelo*
>
> Alicia viene a las seis. (David y Rita)
> David y Rita vienen a las seis.

2 **Consejos (Advice)** Some people are not doing what they should. Say what they have to do. Repeat the correct response after the speaker. (6 *items*)

> *modelo*
>
> Elena no trabaja.
> Elena tiene que trabajar.

3 **Preguntas** Answer each question you hear using the cue in your lab manual. Repeat the correct answer after the speaker.

> *modelo*
>
> ¿Tienen sueño los niños? (no)
> No, los niños no tienen sueño.

1. sí, (yo)   3. no, (nosotros)   5. sí, (mi abuela)   7. el domingo

2. Roberto   4. sí, dos, (yo)   6. mis tíos

4 **Situaciones** Listen to each situation and choose the appropriate **tener** expression. Each situation will be repeated.

1. a. Tienes sueño.   b. Tienes prisa.
2. a. Tienen mucho cuidado.   b. Tienen hambre.
3. a. Tenemos mucho calor.   b. Tenemos mucho frío.
4. a. Tengo sed.   b. Tengo hambre.
5. a. Ella tiene razón.   b. Ella no tiene razón.
6. a. Tengo miedo.   b. Tengo sueño.

5 **Mi familia** Listen to the following description. Then read the statements in your lab manual and decide whether they are **cierto** or **falso**.

	Cierto	Falso		Cierto	Falso
1. Francisco desea ser periodista.	○	○	4. Él tiene una familia pequeña.	○	○
2. Francisco tiene 20 años.	○	○	5. Su madre es ingeniera.	○	○
3. Francisco vive con su familia.	○	○	6. Francisco tiene una hermana mayor.	○	○

vocabulario

You will now hear the vocabulary found in your textbook on the last page of this lesson. Listen and repeat each Spanish word or phrase after the speaker.

© 2016 by Vista Higher Learning, Inc. All rights reserved.

contextos

1   Lugares You will hear six people describe what they are doing. Choose the place that corresponds to the activity.

1. _____   a. el museo   e. el estadio

2. _____   b. el café   f. las montañas

3. _____   c. la piscina   g. el parque

4. _____   d. el cine   h. la biblioteca

5. _____

6. _____

2   Describir For each drawing, you will hear two statements. Choose the one that corresponds to the drawing.

1. a.   b.   2. a.   b.

3. a.   b.   4. a.   b.

3   Completar Listen to this description and write the missing words in your lab manual.

Chapultepec es un (1) _____ muy grande en el (2) _____ de

la (3) _____ de México. Los (4) _____ muchas

(5) _____ llegan a Chapultepec a pasear, descansar y practicar

(6) _____ como (*like*) el (7) _____, el fútbol, el vóleibol y

el (8) _____. Muchos turistas también (9) _____ por

Chapultepec. Visitan los (10) _____ y el (11) _____ a los

Niños Héroes.

© 2016 by Vista Higher Learning, Inc. All rights reserved.   **Lección 4** Lab Activities   **19**

pronunciación

Word stress and accent marks

Every Spanish syllable contains at least one vowel. When two vowels are joined in the same syllable, they form a diphthong. A monosyllable is a word formed by a single syllable.

| pe - **lí** - cu - la | e - di - fi - c**io** | ve**r** | **yo** |

The syllable of a Spanish word that is pronounced most emphatically is the "stressed" syllable.

| bi - blio - **te** - ca | vi - si - **tar** | **par** - que | **fút** - bol |

Words that end in **n**, **s**, or a **vowel** are usually stressed on the next-to-last syllable.

| pe - **lo** - ta | pis - **ci** - na | **ra** - tos | **ha** - blan |

If words that end in **n**, **s**, or a **vowel** are stressed on the last syllable, they must carry an accent mark on the stressed syllable.

| na - ta - **ción** | pa - **pá** | in - **glés** | Jo - **sé** |

Words that do not end in **n**, **s**, or a **vowel** are usually stressed on the last syllable.

| bai - **lar** | es - pa - **ñol** | u - ni - ver - si - **dad** | tra - ba - ja - **dor** |

If words that do not end in **n**, **s**, or a **vowel** are stressed on the next-to-last syllable, they must carry an accent mark on the stressed syllable.

| **béis** - bol | **lá** - piz | **ár** - bol | **Gó** - mez |

---

1 **Práctica** Repeat each word after the speaker, stressing the correct syllable.

1. profesor
2. Puebla
3. ¿Cuántos?
4. Mazatlán
5. examen
6. ¿Cómo?
7. niños
8. Guadalajara
9. programador
10. México
11. están
12. geografía

---

2 **Conversación** Repeat the conversation after the speaker to practice word stress.

MARINA Hola, Carlos. ¿Qué tal?
CARLOS Bien. Oye, ¿a qué hora es el partido de fútbol?
MARINA Creo que es a las siete.
CARLOS ¿Quieres ir?
MARINA Lo siento, pero no puedo. Tengo que estudiar biología.

---

3 **Refranes** Repeat each saying after the speaker to practice word stress.

1. Quien ríe de último, ríe mejor.
2. En la unión está la fuerza.

---

4 **Dictado** You will hear six sentences. Each will be said twice. Listen carefully and write what you hear.

1. _____
2. _____
3. _____
4. _____
5. _____
6. _____

  © 2016 by Vista Higher Learning, Inc. All rights reserved.

estructura

4.1 Present tense of **ir**

1   **Identificar** Listen to each sentence and mark an **X** in the column for the subject of the verb you hear.

> **modelo**
>
> *You hear:* Van a ver una película.
> *You mark:* an **X** under **ellos/ellas**.

	yo	tú	él/ella	nosotros/as	ellos/ellas
Modelo	___	___	___	___	**X** ___
1.	___	___	___	___	___
2.	___	___	___	___	___
3.	___	___	___	___	___
4.	___	___	___	___	___
5.	___	___	___	___	___
6.	___	___	___	___	___

2   **Cambiar** Form a new sentence using the cue you hear as the subject. Repeat the correct answer after the speaker. (*8 items*)

> **modelo**
>
> Ustedes van al Museo Frida Kahlo. (yo)
> *Yo voy al Museo Frida Kahlo.*

3   **Preguntas** Answer each question you hear using the cue in your lab manual. Repeat the correct response after the speaker.

> **modelo**
>
> *You hear:* ¿Quiénes van a la piscina?
> *You see:* Gustavo y Elisa
> *You say:* Gustavo y Elisa van a la piscina.

1. mis amigos   3. al partido de baloncesto   5. sí
2. en el Café Tacuba   4. no   6. pasear en bicicleta

4   **¡Vamos!** Listen to this conversation. Then read the statements in your lab manual and decide whether they are **cierto** or **falso**.

	Cierto	Falso
1. Claudia va a ir al gimnasio.	○	○
2. Claudia necesita comprar una mochila.	○	○
3. Sergio va a visitar a su tía.	○	○
4. Sergio va al gimnasio a las ocho de la noche.	○	○
5. Sergio va a ir al cine a las seis.	○	○
6. Claudia y Sergio van a ver una película.	○	○

© 2016 by Vista Higher Learning, Inc. All rights reserved.

Lección 4 Lab Activities   **21**

4.2 Stem-changing verbs: e→ie, o→ue

1 Identificar Listen to each sentence and write the infinitive form of the verb you hear.

> **modelo**
> You hear: No entiendo el problema.
> You write: *entender*

1. _____   4. _____   7. _____

2. _____   5. _____   8. _____

3. _____   6. _____

2 Preguntas Answer each question you hear using the cue in your lab manual. Repeat the correct response after the speaker.

> **modelo**
> You hear: ¿A qué hora comienza el partido?
> You see: 2:15 p.m.
> You say: *El partido comienza a las dos y cuarto de la tarde.*

1. el jueves, (nosotros)   3. sí   5. leer una revista, (yo)   7. a las tres, (nosotros)

2. no, (yo)   4. sí, (ustedes)   6. mirar la televisión   8. Samuel

3 Diversiones Look at these listings from the entertainment section in a newspaper. Then listen to the questions and write the answers in your lab manual.

23D

MÚSICA

Palacio de Bellas Artes
Ballet folclórico
Viernes 9, 8:30 p.m.

Bosque de Chapultepec
Concierto de música mexicana
Domingo, 1:00 p.m.

MUSEOS
Museo de Arte Moderno

Pinturas de José Clemente
Orozco
De martes a domingo,
de 10:00 a.m. a 6:00 p.m.
Entrada libre

DEPORTES
Copa Internacional de Fútbol
México vs. Guatemala
Estadio Martín
Viernes 9, 8:30 p.m.

Campeonato de baloncesto
Los Universitarios vs. Los Toros
Gimnasio Municipal
Sábado 10, 7:30 p.m.

Torneo de Golf
con Lee Treviño
Club de Golf Atlas
Domingo 8, 9:00 a.m.

1. _____

2. _____

3. _____

4. _____

5. _____

    © 2016 by Vista Higher Learning, Inc. All rights reserved.

4.3 Stem-changing verbs: e→i

1 **Completar** Listen to this radio broadcast and fill in the missing words.

Este fin de semana los excursionistas (*hikers*) (1) _____ más senderos (*trails*).

Dicen que ir de (2) _____ a las montañas es una (3) _____

muy popular y (4) _____ que (5) _____ más senderos. Si lo

(6) _____, la gente va a (7) _____ muy feliz. Si no, ustedes

pueden (8) _____ la historia aquí, en Radio Montaña.

2 **Escoger** Listen to each question and choose the most logical response.

1. a. Normalmente pido tacos.   b. Voy al restaurante los lunes.
2. a. Consigo novelas en la biblioteca.   b. Consigo revistas en el centro.
3. a. Repiten la película el sábado.   b. No deseo ver la película.
4. a. Sigue un programa de baloncesto.   b. No, prefiere bucear.
5. a. Nunca pido pizza.   b. Nunca pido perdón.
6. a. Prefiere visitar un monumento.   b. Prefiere buscar en la biblioteca.
7. a. ¿Quién fue el primer presidente?   b. A las cuatro de la tarde.
8. a. Sí, es muy interesante.   b. Sí, mi hermano juega.

3 **Conversación** Listen to the conversation and answer the questions.

1. ¿Qué quiere Paola?

_____

2. ¿Por qué repite Paola las palabras?

_____

3. ¿Hace Miguel el favor que pide Paola?

_____

4. ¿Dónde puede conseguir la revista?

_____

© 2016 by Vista Higher Learning, Inc. All rights reserved.

4.4 Verbs with irregular **yo** forms

1   **Describir**   For each drawing, you will hear two statements. Choose the one that corresponds to the drawing.

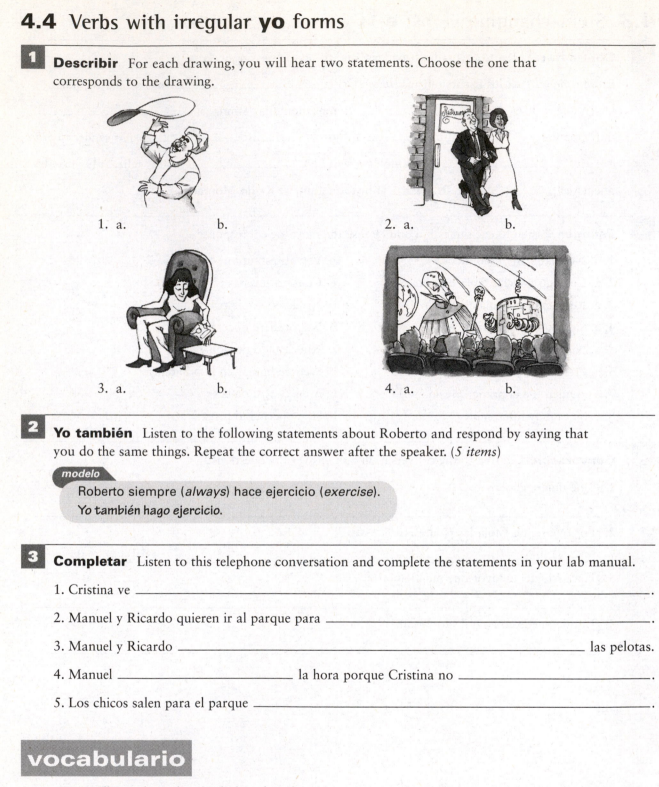

1. a.   b.   2. a.   b.

3. a.   b.   4. a.   b.

2   **Yo también**   Listen to the following statements about Roberto and respond by saying that you do the same things. Repeat the correct answer after the speaker. (*5 items*)

> **modelo**
>
> Roberto siempre (*always*) hace ejercicio (*exercise*).
> *Yo también hago ejercicio.*

3   **Completar**   Listen to this telephone conversation and complete the statements in your lab manual.

1. Cristina ve _____.

2. Manuel y Ricardo quieren ir al parque para _____.

3. Manuel y Ricardo _____ las pelotas.

4. Manuel _____ la hora porque Cristina no _____.

5. Los chicos salen para el parque _____.

vocabulario

You will now hear the vocabulary found in your textbook on the last page of this lesson. Listen and repeat each Spanish word or phrase after the speaker.

       © 2016 by Vista Higher Learning, Inc. All rights reserved.

contextos

Lección 5

1 Identificar You will hear a series of words. Write the word that does not belong in each series.

1. _____   5. _____

2. _____   6. _____

3. _____   7. _____

4. _____   8. _____

2 Describir For each drawing, you will hear two statements. Choose the one that corresponds to the drawing.

1. a. _____ b. _____   2. a. _____ b. _____   3. a. _____ b. _____

3 En la agencia de viajes Listen to this conversation between Mr. Vega and a travel agent. Then read the statements in your lab manual and decide whether they are **cierto** or **falso**.

	Cierto	Falso
1. El señor Vega quiere esquiar, pescar y bucear.	○	○
2. El señor Vega va a Puerto Rico.	○	○
3. El señor Vega quiere ir de vacaciones la primera semana de mayo.	○	○
4. Una habitación en Las Tres Palmas cuesta (*costs*) $85,00.	○	○
5. El hotel tiene restaurante, piscina y *jacuzzi*.	○	○

4 Escoger Listen to each statement and choose the most appropriate activity for that weather condition.

1. a. Vamos a ir a la piscina.   b. Vamos a poner la televisión.

2. a. Voy a escribir una carta.   b. Voy a bucear.

3. a. Vamos al museo.   b. Vamos a tomar el sol.

4. a. Mañana voy a pasear en bicicleta.   b. Mañana voy a esquiar.

5. a. Queremos ir al cine.   b. Queremos nadar.

6. a. Voy a correr en el parque.   b. Voy a leer un libro.

7. a. Quiero escuchar música.   b. Quiero jugar al golf.

© 2016 by Vista Higher Learning, Inc. All rights reserved.

pronunciación

Spanish **b** and **v**

There is no difference in pronunciation between the Spanish letters **b** and **v**. However, each letter can be pronounced two different ways, depending on which letters appear next to them.

    bueno   **v**ólei**b**ol   **bib**lioteca   **v**ivir

B and **v** are pronounced like the English hard **b** when they appear either as the first letter of a word, at the beginning of a phrase, or after **m** or **n**.

    bonito   **v**iajar   tam**b**ién   in**v**estigar

In all other positions, **b** and **v** have a softer pronunciation, which has no equivalent in English. Unlike the hard **b**, which is produced by tightly closing the lips and stopping the flow of air, the soft **b** is produced by keeping the lips slightly open.

    de**b**er   no**v**io   a**b**ril   cer**v**eza

In both pronunciations, there is no difference in sound between **b** and **v**. The English *v* sound, produced by friction between the upper teeth and lower lip, does not exist in Spanish. Instead, the soft **b** comes from friction between the two lips.

    bola   **v**ela   Cari**b**e   decli**v**e

When **b** or **v** begins a word, its pronunciation depends on the previous word. At the beginning of a phrase or after a word that ends in **m** or **n**, it is pronounced as a hard **b**.

    Verónica y su esposo cantan ‿**b**oleros.

Words that begin with **b** or **v** are pronounced with a soft **b** if they appear immediately after a word that ends in a vowel or any consonant other than **m** or **n**.

    Benito es de ‿**B**oquerón pero ‿**v**ive en ‿**V**ictoria.

---

1   **Práctica** Repeat these words after the speaker to practice the **b** and the **v**.

1. hablamos	4. van	7. doble	10. nublado
2. trabajar	5. contabilidad	8. novia	11. llave
3. botones	6. bien	9. béisbol	12. invierno

---

2   **Oraciones** When you hear the number, read the corresponding sentence aloud, focusing on the **b** and **v** sounds. Then listen to the speaker and repeat the sentence.

1. Vamos a Guaynabo en autobús.
2. Voy de vacaciones a la Isla Culebra.
3. Tengo una habitación individual en el octavo piso.
4. Víctor y Eva van por avión al Caribe.
5. La planta baja es bonita también.
6. ¿Qué vamos a ver en Bayamón?
7. Beatriz, la novia de Víctor, es de Arecibo, Puerto Rico.

---

3   **Refranes** Repeat each saying after the speaker to practice the **b** and the **v**.

1. No hay mal que por bien no venga.   2. Hombre prevenido vale por dos.

---

4   **Dictado** You will hear four sentences. Each will be said twice. Listen carefully and write what you hear.

1. _____
2. _____
3. _____
4. _____

© 2016 by Vista Higher Learning, Inc. All rights reserved.

estructura

5.1 Estar with conditions and emotions

1 **Describir** For each drawing, you will hear two statements. Choose the one that corresponds to the drawing.

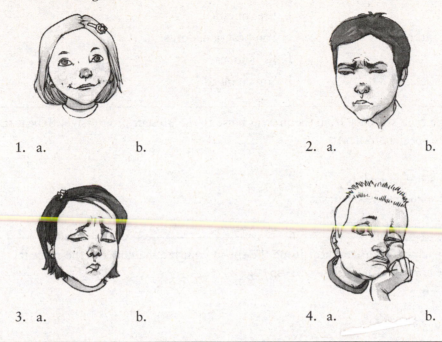

1. a. _____ b. _____   2. a. _____ b. _____

3. a. _____ b. _____   4. a. _____ b. _____

2 **Cambiar** Form a new sentence using the cue you hear as the subject. Repeat the correct answer after the speaker. (8 items)

> **modelo**
> Rubén está enojado con Patricia. (mamá)
> Mamá está enojada con Patricia.

3 **Preguntas** Answer each question you hear using the cues in your lab manual. Repeat the correct response after the speaker.

> **modelo**
> You hear: ¿Está triste Tomás?
> You see: no / contento/a
> You say: No, Tomás está contento.

1. no / abierto/a   3. su hermano   5. no / sucio/a
2. sí, (nosotros)   4. no / ordenado/a   6. estar de vacaciones, (yo)

4 **Situaciones** You will hear four brief conversations. Choose the statement that expresses how the people feel in each situation.

1. a. Ricardo está nervioso.   b. Ricardo está cansado.
2. a. La señora Fuentes está contenta.   b. La señora Fuentes está preocupada.
3. a. Eugenio está aburrido.   b. Eugenio está avergonzado.
4. a. Rosario y Alonso están equivocados.   b. Rosario y Alonso están enojados.

5.2 The present progressive

1 **Escoger** Listen to what these people are doing. Then read the statements in your lab manual and choose the appropriate description.

1. a. Es profesor.   b. Es estudiante.

2. a. Es botones.   b. Es inspector de aduanas.

3. a. Eres artista.   b. Eres huésped.

4. a. Son jugadoras de fútbol.   b. Son programadoras.

5. a. Es ingeniero.   b. Es botones.

6. a. Son turistas.   b. Son empleados.

2 **Transformar** Change each sentence from the present tense to the present progressive. Repeat the correct answer after the speaker. (6 *items*)

> *modelo*
>
> Adriana confirma su reservación.
> Adriana está confirmando su reservación.

3 **Preguntas** Answer each question you hear using the cue in your lab manual and the present progressive. Repeat the correct response after the speaker.

> *modelo*
>
> *You hear:* ¿Qué hacen ellos?
> *You see:* jugar a las cartas
> *You say:* Ellos están jugando a las cartas.

1. hacer las maletas   3. dormir   5. hablar con el botones

2. pescar en el mar   4. correr en el parque   6. comer en el café

4 **Describir** You will hear some questions. Look at the drawing and respond to each question. Repeat the correct answer after the speaker. (6 *items*)

5.3 Ser and estar

1 **Escoger** You will hear some questions with a beep in place of the verb. Decide which form of **ser** or **estar** should complete each question and circle it.

> **modelo**
>
> *You hear:* ¿Cómo (*beep*)?
> *You circle:* **estás** because the question is **¿Cómo estás?**

1. es   está
2. Son   Están
3. Es   Está
4. Es   Está
5. Es   Está
6. Es   Está

2 **¿Cómo es?** You just met Rosa Beltrán at a party. Describe her to a friend by using **ser** or **estar** with the cues you hear. Repeat the correct response after the speaker. (*6 items*)

> **modelo**
>
> muy amable
> *Rosa es muy amable.*

3 **¿Ser o estar?** You will hear the subject of a sentence. Complete the sentence using a form of **ser** or **estar** and the cue in your lab manual. Repeat the correct response after the speaker.

> **modelo**
>
> *You hear:* Papá
> *You see:* en San Juan
> *You say:* Papá está en San Juan.

1. inspector de aduanas
2. la estación de tren
3. a las diez
4. ocupados
5. el 14 de febrero
6. corriendo a clase

4 **¿Lógico o no?** You will hear some statements. Decide if they are **lógico** or **ilógico**.

1. Lógico   Ilógico
2. Lógico   Ilógico
3. Lógico   Ilógico
4. Lógico   Ilógico
5. Lógico   Ilógico
6. Lógico   Ilógico

5 **Ponce** Listen to Carolina's description of her vacation and answer the questions in your lab manual.

1. ¿Dónde está Ponce?

_____

2. ¿Qué tiempo está haciendo?

_____

3. ¿Qué es el Parque de Bombas?

_____

4. ¿Que día es hoy?

_____

5. ¿Por qué no va Carolina al Parque de Bombas hoy?

_____

5.4 Direct object nouns and pronouns

1 **Escoger** Listen to each question and choose the most logical response.

1. a. Sí, voy a comprarlo.
   b. No, no voy a comprarla.

2. a. Joaquín lo tiene.
   b. Joaquín la tiene.

3. a. Sí, los puedo llevar.
   b. No, no te puedo llevar.

4. a. Irene los tiene.
   b. Irene las tiene.

5. a. Sí, te llevamos al partido.
   b. Sí, nos llevas al partido.

6. a. No, vamos a hacerlo mañana.
   b. No, vamos a hacerla mañana.

7. a. Va a conseguirlos mañana.
   b. Va a conseguirlas mañana.

8. a. Pienso visitarla el fin de semana.
   b. Pienso visitarte el fin de semana.

2 **Cambiar** Restate each sentence you hear using a direct object pronoun. Repeat the correct answer after the speaker. (*6 items*)

> **modelo**
> Isabel está mirando la televisión.
> *Isabel está mirándola.*

Isabel está mirando la televisión con Diego.

3 **No veo nada** You just broke your glasses and now you can't see anything. Respond to each statement using a direct object pronoun. Repeat the correct answer after the speaker. (*6 items*)

> **modelo**
> Allí está el Museo de Arte e Historia.
> *¿Dónde? No lo veo.*

4 **Preguntas** Answer each question you hear in the negative. Repeat the correct response after the speaker. (*6 items*)

> **modelo**
> ¿Haces tu maleta?
> *No, no la hago.*

vocabulario

You will now hear the vocabulary found in your textbook on the last page of this lesson. Listen and repeat each Spanish word or phrase after the speaker.

© 2016 by Vista Higher Learning, Inc. All rights reserved.

contextos

1 **¿Lógico o ilógico?** Listen to each statement and indicate if it is **lógico** or **ilógico**.

1. Lógico	Ilógico		5. Lógico	Ilógico
2. Lógico	Ilógico		6. Lógico	Ilógico
3. Lógico	Ilógico		7. Lógico	Ilógico
4. Lógico	Ilógico		8. Lógico	Ilógico

2 **Escoger** Listen as each person talks about the clothing he or she needs to buy. Then choose the activity for which the clothing would be appropriate.

1. a. ir a la playa   b. ir al cine

2. a. jugar al golf   b. buscar trabajo (*work*)

3. a. salir a bailar   b. ir a las montañas

4. a. montar a caballo   b. jugar a las cartas

5. a. jugar al vóleibol   b. comer en un restaurante elegante

6. a. hacer un viaje   b. patinar en línea

3 **Preguntas** Respond to each question saying that the opposite is true. Repeat the correct answer after the speaker. (6 *items*)

> **modelo**
>
> Las sandalias cuestan mucho, ¿no?
> No, las sandalias cuestan poco.

4 **Describir** You will hear some questions. Look at the drawing and write the answer to each question.

Diana   Carmen

1. _____

2. _____

3. _____

4. _____

© 2016 by Vista Higher Learning, Inc. All rights reserved.

pronunciación

The consonants **d** and **t**

Like **b** and **v**, the Spanish **d** can have a hard sound or a soft sound, depending on which letters appear next to it.

    ¿**D**ónde?   ven**d**er   na**d**ar   ver**dad**

At the beginning of a phrase and after **n** or **l**, the letter **d** is pronounced with a hard sound. This sound is similar to the English *d* in *dog*, but a little softer and duller. The tongue should touch the back of the upper teeth, not the roof of the mouth.

    Don   **d**inero   tien**d**a   fal**d**a

In all other positions, **d** has a soft sound. It is similar to the English *th* in *there*, but a little softer.

    me**d**ias   ver**d**e   vesti**d**o   huéspe**d**

When **d** begins a word, its pronunciation depends on the previous word. At the beginning of a phrase or after a word that ends in **n** or **l**, it is pronounced as a hard **d**.

    Don **D**iego no tiene el **d**iccionario.

Words that begin with **d** are pronounced with a soft **d** if they appear immediately after a word that ends in a vowel or any consonant other than **n** or **l**.

    Doña **D**olores es **d**e la capital.

When pronouncing the Spanish **t**, the tongue should touch the back of the upper teeth, not the roof of the mouth. In contrast to the English *t*, no air is expelled from the mouth.

    traje   pan**t**alones   **t**arje**t**a   **t**ienda

1   **Práctica** Repeat each phrase after the speaker to practice the **d** and the **t**.

1. Hasta pronto.	5. No hay de qué.	9. Es estupendo.
2. De nada.	6. ¿De dónde es usted?	10. No tengo computadora.
3. Mucho gusto.	7. ¡Todos a bordo!	11. ¿Cuándo vienen?
4. Lo siento.	8. No puedo.	12. Son las tres y media.

2   **Oraciones** When you hear the number, read the corresponding sentence aloud, focusing on the **d** and **t** sounds. Then listen to the speaker and repeat the sentence.

1. Don Teodoro tiene una tienda en un almacén en La Habana.
2. Don Teodoro vende muchos trajes, vestidos y zapatos todos los días.
3. Un día un turista, Federico Machado, entra en la tienda para comprar un par de botas.
4. Federico regatea con don Teodoro y compra las botas y también un par de sandalias.

3   **Refranes** Repeat each saying after the speaker to practice the **d** and the **t**.

1. En la variedad está el gusto.   2. Aunque la mona se vista de seda, mona se queda.

4   **Dictado** You will hear four sentences. Each will be said twice. Listen carefully and write what you hear.

1. _____
2. _____
3. _____
4. _____

© 2016 by Vista Higher Learning, Inc. All rights reserved.

estructura

6.1 Saber and conocer

1 **¿Saber o conocer?** You will hear some sentences with a beep in place of the verb. Decide which form of **saber** or **conocer** should complete each sentence and circle it.

> **modelo**
>
> You hear: (Beep) cantar.
> You circle: **Sé** because the sentence is **Sé cantar**.

| 1. Sé | Conozco | 3. Sabemos | Conocemos | 5. Sabes | Conoces |
| 2. Saben | Conocen | 4. Sé | Conozco | 6. Sabes | Conoces |

2 **Cambiar** Listen to the following statements and say that you do the same activities. Repeat the correct answer after the speaker. (5 items)

> **modelo**
>
> Julia sabe nadar.
> Yo también sé nadar.

3 **Preguntas** Answer each question using the cue you hear. Repeat the correct response after the speaker. (6 items)

> **modelo**
>
> ¿Conocen tus padres Antigua? (Sí)
> Sí, mis padres conocen Antigua.

4 **Mi compañera de cuarto** Listen as Jennifer describes her roommate. Then read the statements in your lab manual and decide whether they are **cierto** or **falso**.

	Cierto	Falso
1. Jennifer conoció (met) a Laura en la escuela primaria.	O	O
2. Laura sabe hacer muchas cosas.	O	O
3. Laura sabe hablar alemán.	O	O
4. Laura sabe buscar gangas.	O	O
5. Laura sabe patinar en línea.	O	O
6. Laura conoce a algunos muchachos simpáticos.	O	O

5 **De compras** Listen to this conversation between Carmen and Rosalía. Then choose the correct answers to the questions in your lab manual.

1. ¿Cuál es el problema de Carmen cuando va de compras?
   a. Siempre encuentra gangas.   b. Nunca encuentra ofertas.
2. ¿Conoce Carmen el nuevo centro comercial?
   a. No lo conoce, pero sabe dónde está.   b. Ni lo conoce, ni sabe dónde está.
3. ¿Qué quiere comprar Rosalía en el centro comercial?
   a. Quiere comprar zapatos.   b. No quiere comprar nada.
4. ¿Cuándo van Carmen y Rosalía de compras?
   a. Mañana antes del trabajo.   b. Mañana después del trabajo.

© 2016 by Vista Higher Learning, Inc. All rights reserved.

6.2 Indirect object pronouns

1 **Escoger** Listen to each question and choose the most logical response.

1. a. Sí, le muestro el abrigo.

   b. Sí, me muestra el abrigo.

2. a. No, no le presto el suéter azul.

   b. No, no te presto el suéter azul.

3. a. Voy a comprarles ropa interior.

   b. Vamos a comprarle ropa interior.

4. a. Sí, nos dan las nuevas sandalias.

   b. Sí, me dan las nuevas sandalias.

5. a. Nos cuestan veinte dólares.

   b. Les cuestan veinte dólares.

6. a. Sí, nos trae un sombrero.

   b. Sí, te traigo un sombrero.

2 **Transformar** Cecilia is shopping. Say for whom she buys these items using indirect object pronouns. Repeat the correct answer after the speaker. (6 *items*)

> *modelo*
> Cecilia compra una bolsa para Dora.
> *Cecilia le compra una bolsa.*

3 **Preguntas** Answer each question you hear using the cue in your lab manual. Repeat the correct response after the speaker.

> *modelo*
> *You hear:* ¿Quién está esperándote?
> *You see:* Mauricio
> *You say: Mauricio está esperándome.*

1. sí	3. no	5. Antonio
2. $50,00	4. su traje nuevo	6. bluejeans

4 **En el centro comercial** Listen to this conversation and answer the questions in your lab manual.

1. ¿Quién es Gustavo?

   _____

2. ¿Qué está haciendo Gustavo?

   _____

3. ¿Qué le pregunta Gustavo a José?

   _____

4. ¿Por qué le presta dinero José?

   _____

5. ¿Cuándo va a regalarle (*to give*) la falda a Norma?

   _____

 © 2016 by Vista Higher Learning, Inc. All rights reserved.

6.3 Preterite tense of regular verbs

1 **Identificar** Listen to each sentence and decide whether the verb is in the present or the preterite tense. Mark an **X** in the appropriate column.

> **modelo**
> You hear: Alejandro llevó un suéter marrón.
> You mark: an **X** under **Preterite**.

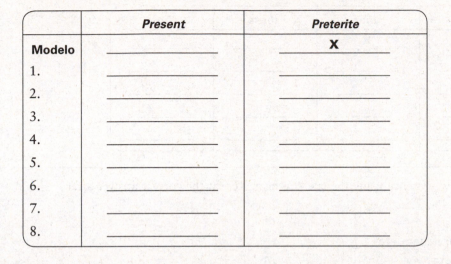

	Present	Preterite
Modelo	_____	X _____
1.	_____	_____
2.	_____	_____
3.	_____	_____
4.	_____	_____
5.	_____	_____
6.	_____	_____
7.	_____	_____
8.	_____	_____

2 **Cambiar** Change each sentence from the present to the preterite. Repeat the correct answer after the speaker. (*8 items*)

> **modelo**
> Compro unas sandalias baratas.
> *Compré unas sandalias baratas.*

3 **Preguntas** Answer each question you hear using the cue in your lab manual. Repeat the correct response after the speaker.

> **modelo**
> You hear: ¿Dónde conseguiste tus botas?
> You see: en la tienda Lacayo
> You say: *Conseguí mis botas en la tienda Lacayo.*

1. $26,00   2. ayer   3. Marta   4. no   5. no   6. no

4 **¿Estás listo?** Listen to this conversation between Matilde and Hernán. Make a list of the tasks Hernán has already done in preparation for his trip and a list of the tasks he still needs to do.

Tareas completadas   **Tareas que necesita hacer**

_____   _____

_____   _____

_____   _____

_____   _____

© 2016 by Vista Higher Learning, Inc. All rights reserved.   **Lección 6** Lab Activities

6.4 Demonstrative adjectives and pronouns

1 **En el mercado** A group of tourists is shopping at an open-air market. Listen to what they say, and mark an **X** in the column for the demonstrative adjective you hear.

> *modelo*
> *You hear:* Me gusta mucho esa bolsa.
> *You mark:* an **X** under *that*.

	this	*that*	*these*	*those*
Modelo	_____	X ____	_____	_____
1.	_____	_____	_____	_____
2.	_____	_____	_____	_____
3.	_____	_____	_____	_____
4.	_____	_____	_____	_____

2 **Cambiar** Form a new sentence using the cue you hear. Repeat the correct answer after the speaker. (*6 items*)

> *modelo*
> Quiero este suéter. (chaqueta)
> *Quiero esta chaqueta.*

3 **Transformar** Form a new sentence using the cue you hear. Repeat the correct answer after the speaker. (*6 items*)

> *modelo*
> Aquel abrigo es muy hermoso. (corbatas)
> *Aquellas corbatas son muy hermosas.*

4 **Preguntas** Answer each question you hear in the negative using a form of the demonstrative pronoun **ése**. Repeat the correct response after the speaker. (*8 items*)

> *modelo*
> ¿Quieres esta blusa?
> *No, no quiero ésa.*

5 **De compras** Listen to this conversation. Then read the statements in your lab manual and decide whether they are **cierto** or **falso**.

	Cierto	Falso
1. Flor quiere ir al almacén Don Guapo.	○	○
2. Enrique trabaja en el almacén Don Guapo.	○	○
3. El centro comercial está lejos de los chicos.	○	○
4. Van al almacén que está al lado del Hotel Plaza.	○	○

vocabulario

You will now hear the vocabulary found in your textbook on the last page of this lesson. Listen and repeat each Spanish word or phrase after the speaker.

© 2016 by Vista Higher Learning, Inc. All rights reserved.